LEONARDO
DA VINCI

PHAIDON

LUDWIG GOLDSCHEIDER

LEONARDO

LIFE AND WORK

WITH THE LEONARDO BIOGRAPHY
BY VASARI·1568·
NEWLY ANNOTATED·
114 ILLUSTRATIONS
INCLUDING 41 IN COLOUR

DA VINCI

PAINTINGS AND DRAWINGS

PHAIDON PUBLISHERS DISTRIBUTED BY
DOUBLEDAY & COMPANY INC·GARDEN CITY·NEW YORK

© 1959 PHAIDON PRESS LTD · LONDON SW7

MADE IN GREAT BRITAIN

TEXT AND COLOUR PLATES PRINTED BY HUNT BARNARD & CO · LTD · AYLESBURY · BUCKS

PHOTOGRAVURE PLATES PRINTED BY CLARKE & SHERWELL LTD · NORTHAMPTON

BOUND AT THE PITMAN PRESS · BATH

BOOK DESIGN BY THE AUTHOR

CONTENTS

FOREWORD

TO THE FIRST EDITION: 1943

THE present work is not a book on Leonardo. It is rather a book by him.

It contains large-scale reproductions of all his paintings, together with a few which are reasonably ascribed to him; it also reproduces some sculptures, thought to be his; and the best part of the book concerns Leonardo's drawings, most of which are given in their original sizes.

Besides the actual reproductions of Leonardo's work, there is his biography by Vasari, who was a boy of eight when Leonardo died. There is also a number of documents – letters by Leonardo and information by his contemporaries, which combine to show how Leonardo's work appeared to those who lived and worked with him. A systematic bibliography and some notes on the plates will help readers to find their way through the maze of Leonardo discussions, if they are eager or curious enough to wander so far.

Actually, the plates, the documents, the master's biography by Vasari, and the passages from other biographies, enable everyone to make up his own book on Leonardo by reading this one. He will see what Leonardo did, he can study information directly from the Master and from his contemporaries – and he probably does not want more.

It was not originally my intention to put anything of my own into this book; but I have found it necessary to include here several hundred notes, to make the reader acquainted with modern judgments on Leonardo. In these notes I could not help giving also my own opinions and saying a few things that are new. Thus, for instance, I have ventured an explanation of the 'knots', and commented upon the two words on the scroll of the Ambrosiana Musician. Many similar things may be found by an inquirer in the captions, the footnotes, and in the comparative illustrations.

NOTE TO THE SIXTH EDITION

THE text of this edition has been only slightly revised. But the Bibliography has been brought up to date, translations of the two early Leonardo biographies by Paolo Giovio and the Anonimo Gaddiano are now included, the footnotes have been augmented, and so has the Chronology.

The format of the book has changed; the size of the illustrations has, on the whole, remained the same. The selection of plates is now somewhat different; quite a number of new details are shown (e.g. 60–62, 74, 77–79, 86–90, 95, etc.); on the other hand, several well-known drawings had to be left out. (All of them can be found in the volumes of Bodmer and Popham.)

Some readers – though probably not always agreeing with my chronology – will regret that the plates are not arranged in chronological order. However, for a popular book, meant to serve as a first introduction to Leonardo's art, a different arrangement appears to be better suited.

In the Notes to the Plates I have taken care to say which paintings and drawings are not generally accepted as by Leonardo. (Therefore these notes and the bibliography are supplementary each to the other.) I have also pointed out which paintings are damaged and which drawings retouched by a later hand. All the works reproduced in the present volume I know from autopsy.

London, 1959

L.G.

LIFE OF LEONARDO DA VINCI
PAINTER AND SCULPTOR OF FLORENCE
BY GIORGIO VASARI · 1568

LIONARDO DA VINCI

LIONARDO DA VINCI PITT.
E SCVLTOR FIOR.

VITA DI LIONARDO DA VINCI
PITTORE, ET SCVLTORE
FIORENTINO.

THE heavens often rain down the richest gifts on human beings naturally, but sometimes with lavish abundance bestow upon a single individual beauty, grace and ability, so that whatever he does, every action is so divine that he distances all other men, and clearly displays how his genius is the gift of God and not an acquirement of human art. Men saw this in Leonardo da Vinci, whose personal beauty could not be exaggerated, whose every movement was grace itself and whose abilities were so extraordinary that he could readily solve every difficulty. He possessed great physical strength, combined with dexterity, and a spirit and courage invariably royal and magnanimous; and the fame of his name increased not only during his lifetime but also after his death.

This marvellous and divine Leonardo was the son of Ser Piero da Vinci.[1] He would have made great

1. The little town of Vinci is situated in Tuscany between Empoli and Pistoia, about 20 miles from Florence. Vasari calls Leonardo's father 'Ser' Piero, a title borne by notaries. Ser Piero was engaged from 1451 onwards in his profession, mainly in Florence, where he became one of the most sought-after notaries. Leonardo, the illegitimate son of Ser Piero and the peasant maid, Caterina, was born on the 15th of April, 1452. Caterina lived at Anchiano, a hamlet outside Vinci. She married some peasant when Leonardo was five, and the child was received into his father's household where he was taken care of by a young, childless stepmother. (Ser Piero had married a rich girl aged sixteen, in the year Leonardo was born. By his third and fourth wives Ser Piero had eleven children.)

Portrait of Verrochio, by Lorenzo di Credi, c. 1485. Florence, Uffizi.
Leonardo was Verrocchio's pupil; but his favourite disciple and the executor of his
will was Lorenzo di Credi, who finished for him the Pistoia altar-piece
and other works.

profit in learning had he not been so capricious and fickle, for he began to learn many things and then gave them up. [2] Thus in arithmetic, during the few months that he studied it, he made such progress that he frequently confounded his master by continually raising doubts and difficulties. [3] He devoted

2. Paolo Giovio, in his short biography of Leonardo, written in about 1527, judged similarly but more comprehendingly; after mentioning Leonardo's exertions 'in the sciences and the liberal arts', his optical and anatomical studies, he adds regretfully: 'But while he was thus spending his time in the close investigation of subordinate branches of his art he brought but very few works to completion, for his masterly facility and his fastidious disposition caused him to discard many works he had already begun.' Similar opinions were held by Sieur de Chantelou (who had a share in Du Fresne's edition of Leonardo's *Trattato della Pittura* of 1651). In his *Journal de voyage du chev. Bernin en France* we find, under the date of 24th August 1665, the following conversation. '*Chantelou:* The relationship between Leonardo and Francis I was based entirely on the admiration the King had for him, although Leonardo was rather a speculative thinker than a creative artist. – *Bernini:* What you mean is Leonardo understood how to grow old working endlessly on one single composition. – *Chantelou:* The outcome of this is anyway that France possesses nothing from his hand but a few unfinished paintings. – *Bernini:* Naturally. Leonardo may have taken six years to paint just the hair.'

3. Edward McCurdy assumes that Leonardo's teacher in mathematics was Benedetto dell'Abbaco, the most famous man of his calling in Florence. Leonardo continued to cultivate the study of mathematics all his life, and about 1497 collaborated in *De Divina Proportione*, the work of his friend, Fra Luca Pacioli; the geometrical figures in the 1509 edition are after Leonardo's drawings. Mathematics was for him the foundation of art, and on the back of a drawing (Windsor 19118) he wrote: 'Let no man who is no mathematician read the elements of my work.'

some time to music, and soon learned to play the lyre, and, being filled with a lofty and delicate spirit, he could sing and improvise divinely with it. [4]

Yet though he studied so many different things, he never neglected design and working in relief, those being the things which appealed to his fancy more than any other. When Ser Piero perceived this, and knowing the boy's soaring spirit, he one day took some of his drawings to Andrea del Verrocchio, [5] who was his close friend, and asked his opinion whether Leonardo would do anything by studying design. Andrea was so amazed at these early efforts that he advised Ser Piero to have the boy taught. So it was decided that Leonardo should go to Andrea's workshop. [6] The boy was greatly delighted, and not only practised his profession, but all those in which design has a part. Possessed of a divine and marvellous intellect, and being an excellent geometrician, he not only worked in sculpture, doing out of clay some heads of smiling women, of which casts in plaster are still taken, and children's heads (*teste di putti*), also, executed like a master, [7] but also prepared many architectural plans and elevations, and he was the first, though so young, to propose to canalize the Arno from Pisa to Florence. [8] He made designs for mills, fulling machines, and other engines to go by water, and as painting was to be his profession he studied drawing from life. He would make clay models of figures, draping them with soft rags dipped in plaster, and would then draw them patiently on thin sheets of cambric or linen, in black and white, with the point of the brush. [9] He did these admirably, as may be

4. Paolo Giovio, the Anonimo Gaddiano, Luca Pacioli and Lomazzo, all mention Leonardo's musical talent, a gift which he shared with Piero della Francesca, Giorgione, and his teacher Verrocchio. Paolo Giovio relates: 'He sang beautifully to his own accompaniment on the lyre to the delight of the entire Court of Milan.' The Anonimo Gaddiano (see the Biography on p. 31) says: 'Leonardo was an exquisite musician on the lyre and was the teacher of the singer Atalante Migliorotti.'

5. Andrea del Verrocchio, born in Florence 1435, died in Venice 1488; pupil of Donatello (according to Baldinucci); best known through his bronze equestrian statue of Colleoni in Venice, which was not completed by him (but by Leopardi, 1496, and set up after the master's death).

6. It is uncertain at which date Leonardo was placed with Verrocchio; we only know that as late as 1476 Leonardo was still staying and working with him. Some authorities (including Müller-Walde, Thiis, Van Marle, and Heydenreich) assume that he came to the studio in 1466, when the boy was between fourteen and fifteen years; but others (Ravaisson-Mollien, Richter, Venturi, de Rinaldis, and Valentiner) suggest a date between summer 1469 and spring 1470. As Leonardo is still mentioned in the tax records of Vinci in 1469, the latter date is most probably correct. In July 1472 Leonardo became a member of the Guild of St Luke, as transpires from an entry in 'the red book of the Florence Guild of Painters'. (The usual term of apprenticeship for a painter in those days was six years; but sometimes it was only four, and when Michelangelo was placed with the brothers Ghirlandaio, it was stipulated that the term should be only three years. There is no fixed rule.)

On the 1st January, 1478, Leonardo received his first independent commission; in March, 1481, the contract for the 'Adoration of the Kings' was entered into, and at this time Leonardo was working in his own dwelling, and no longer with Verrocchio. By July, 1481, the model for the equestrian statue of Colleoni was finished in Verrocchio's workshop in Florence. A short time afterwards Leonardo removed to Milan and a few years later Verrocchio to Venice.

7. Lomazzo in his *Treatise on Painting* (Milan, 1584, p. 127) mentions a terracotta head of the infant Christ in his collection, 'by Leonardo's own hand'; also a clay relief of a horse by Leonardo, in the collection of the sculptor Leone Leoni. All these sculptural works of Leonardo's youth are lost, and all we know for certain about Leonardo as a sculptor is based on a few drawings; all the attributions are mere conjectures.

8. The aim of the plan was to procure for Florence direct access to the sea. Numerous drawings connected with this idea have been preserved. (Cf. e.g. Richter §§ 1001, 1006; Windsor Catalogue, Nos. 12279, 12659). Leonardo was particularly occupied with this idea in the summer of the year 1503. (See G. B. Venturi, *Essai sur les ouvrages physico-mathemat. de L. da V.*, Paris, 1797, p. 39.)

9. A good and richly illustrated survey of these drapery drawings, which were executed in Verrocchio's studio for study purposes, is to be found in Bernard Berenson's *The Drawings of the Florentine Painters*, amplified edition, Chicago 1938; particularly figs. 517–531. How such drawings were employed in painting is shown by our plate 43. Drapery drawings from clay models were, in the earlier Renaissance, rather usual, and not in Verrocchio's workshop alone. In the life of Piero della Francesca (about 1416–1492), Vasari says: 'Piero was in the habit of making clay models, covering them with soft cloth with a number of folds in order to copy them and turn them to account.' In the *Life of Lorenzo di Credi* Vasari speaks of 'drawings copying clay models draped in waxed cloth'.

seen by specimens in my book of designs. He also drew upon paper so carefully and well that no one has ever equalled him. I have a head in grisaille which is divine. The grace of God so possessed his mind, his memory and intellect formed such a mighty union, and he could so clearly express his ideas in discourse, that he was able to confound the boldest opponents. Every day he made models and designs for the removal of mountains with ease and to pierce them to pass from one place to another, and by means of levers, cranes and winches to raise and draw heavy weights; he devised a method for cleansing ports, and to raise water from great depths, schemes which his brain never ceased to evolve. Many designs for these notions are scattered about, and I have seen numbers of them. He spent much

time in making a regular design of a series of knots so that the cord may be traced from one end to the other, the whole filling a round space. There is a fine engraving of this most difficult design, and in the middle are the words: *Leonardi Vinci Academia*.[10] Among these models and designs there was one which he several times showed to many able citizens who then ruled Florence, of a method of raising the church of San Giovanni and putting steps under it without its falling down. He argued with so much eloquence that it was not until after his departure that they recognized the impossibility of such a feat.

His charming conversation won all hearts, and although he possessed nothing and worked little, he kept servants and horses; of which latter he was very fond, and indeed he loved all animals, and trained them with great kindness and patience. Often, when passing places where birds were sold, he would let them out of their

School of Leonardo: Knot, engraving, c. 1499. London, British Museum. *This 'fantasia dei vinci', a pattern of linked chains, is most probably a hieroglyphic signature of Leonardo.*

cages and having paid the vendor the price asked, he let them fly away into the air, restoring to them the lost liberty. Wherefore Nature favoured him so greatly that in whatever his brain or mind took up he displayed unrivalled harmony, vigour, vivacity, excellence, beauty and grace.

10. Six of these engravings have been preserved. Albrecht Dürer copied them (Richter, vol. I, p. 387, n.). From the inscription on these knots it has been assumed that Leonardo was the director of a drawing academy (school) in Milan, but this supposition is now generally discredited. I should like to put forward the suggestion that these engravings represent tickets for scientific disputations, being either tickets of admission or prize tickets. By 'academia' was understood in the Renaissance a poetical or scientific tourney; 'academia coronaria' was the name of the poetical competition which Leon Battista Alberti organized in the Florence Cathedral on the 22nd October, 1441. Leonardo,

Pacioli, and the Duke were present on 8th February, 1499, at a scientific tourney (*duello*) in the Castello Sforzesco. But why was a knot used as an emblem for Leonardo's 'Academia', and what is the reason for the interlacing ornaments on the dress of Mona Lisa and in other paintings? The explanation is a play on the words *vincire* (to fetter, to lace, to knot) and *Vinci*; being a cryptographic signature of Leonardo da Vinci. Niccola da Correggio, who through Atalante (see note on plate 26) was in connection with Leonardo, designed in 1492 and 1493 dresses for Isabella and Beatrice d'Este with this pattern of interlaced links embroidered on silk.

His knowledge of art, indeed, prevented him from finishing many things which he had begun, for he felt that his hand would be unable to realize the perfect creations of his imagination, as his mind formed such difficult, subtle and marvellous conceptions that his hands, skilful as they were, could never have expressed them. His interests were so numerous that his inquiries into natural phenomena led him to study the properties of herbs and to observe the movements of the heavens, the moon's orbit and the progress of the sun.[11]

LEONARDO was placed, as I have said, with Andrea del Verrocchio in his childhood by Ser Piero, and his master happened to be painting a picture of St John baptizing Christ. For this Leonardo did an angel holding some garments; and, although quite young, he made it far better than the figures of Andrea.[12] The latter would never afterwards touch colours, chagrined that a child should know more than he.

Leonardo was next employed to draw Adam and Eve, sinning in the Earthly Paradise, a cartoon for a door-hanging in tapestry, to be made in Flanders of gold and silk, to be sent to the King of Portugal. Here he did a meadow in grisaille, with the lights in white lead, containing much vegetation and some animals, unsurpassable for finish and naturalness. There is a fig-tree, the leaves and branches beautifully foreshortened and executed with such care that the mind is amazed at the amount of patience displayed. There is also a palm-tree, the rotundity of the dates being executed with great and marvellous art, due to the patience and ingenuity of Leonardo. This work was not carried farther, and the cartoon is now in Florence in the fortunate house of the illustrious Ottaviano de' Medici, to whom it was given not long ago by Leonardo's uncle.[13]

It is said that when Ser Piero was at his country-seat he was requested by a peasant of his estate to get a round panel of wood[14] painted for him at Florence, which he had cut from a fig-tree on his farm. Piero readily consented, as the man was very skilful in catching birds and fishing, and was very useful to him in such matters. Accordingly Piero brought the wood to Florence and asked Leonardo to paint something upon it, without telling him to whom it belonged. Leonardo, on taking it up to examine it one day, found it warped, badly prepared and clumsy, but with the help of fire he made it straight, and giving it to a turner, had it rendered smooth and even instead of being rough and rude. Then, after preparing the surface in his own way by covering it with *gesso*, he began to think about what he should paint on it, and resolved to do the Head of Medusa to terrify all beholders. To a room to which he alone had access, Leonardo took lizards, newts, maggots, snakes, moths, locusts, bats, and

11. In the first edition of Vasari's *Life of Leonardo* (1550) followed here a sentence which is omitted in the second edition: 'Leonardo was of such a heretical frame of mind that he did not adhere to any kind of religion, believing that it was perhaps better to be a philosopher than a Christian.'

12. Albertini's description of Florence, 1510, already mentions Leonardo's share in this painting. (The angel on the left, see plate 43.) Not only the Angel, but also the Landscape (plate 87) has been painted over by Leonardo, and indeed with oil colours above Verrocchio's tempera. (A. Bayersdorfer, *Leben und Schriften*, 1908, pp. 72–76. Bode, *Leonardo-Studien*, 1921, pp. 10–14.) The tuft of grass beside the kneeling angel testifies to the same understanding of the life of plants as Leonardo's later plant studies.

13. Leonardo's father had only one brother, Francesco, who dwelt, as a countryman and silk-worm rearer, in Vinci. Allessandro degli Amadori, a brother of Ser Piero's first wife, also called himself Leonardo's uncle; in 1506 he interpreted to Leonardo the wishes of Isabella d'Este. (Beltrami, Documenti, Nos. 173, 174.) I believe that Messer Allessandro Amadori, Canonico di Fiesole, was the first owner of Leonardo's cartoon of Adam and Eve. This cartoon has disappeared.

Suida surmises that Raphael's 'Fall of Man' in the Stanza della Segnatura of the Vatican is a free rendering of Leonardo's lost cartoon.

14. In the original *rotella*, which in fact means: a shield of a round form.

other animals of the kind, out of which he composed a horrible and terrible monster, of poisonous breath, issuing from a dark and broken rock, belching poison from its open throat, fire from its eyes, and smoke from its nostrils, of truly terrible and horrible aspect. He was so engrossed with the work that he did not notice the terrible stench of the dead animals, being absorbed in his love for art. His father and the peasant no longer asked for the work, and when it was finished Leonardo told his father to send for it when he pleased, as he had done his part. Accordingly Ser Piero went to his rooms one morning to fetch it. When he knocked at the door Leonardo opened it and told him to wait a little, and, returning to his room, put the round panel in the light on his easel, which he turned with its back to the window to make the light dim; then he called his father in. Ser Piero, taken unaware, started back, not thinking of the round piece of wood, or that the face which he saw was painted, and was beating a retreat when Leonardo detained him and said, 'This work is as I wanted it to be; take it away, then, as it is producing the effect intended.' Ser Piero indeed thought it almost a miracle, and he warmly praised Leonardo's idea. He then quietly went and bought another round panel with a heart transfixed by a dart painted upon it, and gave it to the peasant, who was grateful to Piero all his life.

Piero took Leonardo's work secretly to Florence and sold it to some merchants for one hundred ducats, and in a short time it came into the hands of the Duke of Milan, who bought it of them for three hundred ducats.[15]

Leonardo next did a very excellent Madonna, which afterwards belonged to Pope Clement VII. Among other things it contained a bowl of water with some marvellous flowers, the dew upon them seeming actually to be there, so that they looked more real than reality itself.[16] For his good friend Antonio Segni he drew a Neptune on a folio sheet of paper, with so much diligence that it seemed alive.[17] The sea is troubled and his car is drawn by sea-horses, with the sprites, monsters, and south winds; there are in it also some very fine heads of sea-gods. This drawing was given by Antonio's son Fabio to Messer Giovanni Gaddi with this epigram:

Pinxit Virgilius Neptunum, pinxit Homerus,
Dum maris undisoni per vada flectit equos.
Mente quidem vates illum conspexit uterque,
Vincius ast oculis; jureque vincit eos.[18]

Leonardo then had the fancy to paint a picture of the Medusa's head in oils with a garland of snakes about it, the most extraordinary idea imaginable, but as the work required time, it remained unfinished, the fate of nearly all his projects.[19] This is among the treasures in the palace of Duke Cosimo, together

15. Now lost.

16. Some critics identify Leonardo's *Madonna with the Glass Vase full of Flowers* with the painting in Munich, plate 63.

17. For a study to this lost drawing, see plate 46. For Antonio Segni Botticelli painted his *Calumny of Apelles*. Concerning the Gaddi Collection see J. Schlosser, *Ghiberti*, 1941, p. 142.

18. The meaning of this Latin epigram is roughly as follows: 'Virgil and Homer both depicted Neptune driving his sea-horses through the rushing waves. The poets saw him in their imaginations, but Leonardo with his own eyes, and so he rightly surpassed them.' There is a pun on the words *Vincius* (the man from Vinci) and *vincit* (he vanquished) which is untranslatable.

19. Lost. The panel in the Uffizi at Florence, which was once erroneously supposed to be Leonardo's Head of the Medusa, is a work of the 17th century, and actually an adaptation of the head on a shield in the *Fight for the Standard* (cf. plate 108; the fallen man in the centre foreground). But it may be that *The Head of the Medusa* by Rubens in the Vienna Museum (No. 846) is a free version of Leonardo's lost painting.

The Angel of the Annunciation. Detail of a black chalk drawing, corrected
in pen and ink, c. 1506. Windsor Castle, Royal Library (No. 12328).
Drawing by a pupil of Leonardo, with some retouchings by the master.
(Compare also plate 55, which dates from about ten years later.)

with the Head of an Angel, who is raising an arm in the air, this arm being foreshortened from the shoulder to the elbow, while the other rests on its breast.[20]

So marvellous was Leonardo's mind that, desiring to throw his things into greater relief, he endeavoured to obtain greater depths of shadow, and sought the deepest blacks in order to render the lights clearer by contrast. He succeeded so well that his scenes looked rather like representations of the night, there being no bright light, than of the lightness of day, though all was done with the idea of throwing things into greater relief and to find the end and perfection of art.

Leonardo was so delighted when he saw curious heads, whether bearded or hairy, that he would follow about anyone who had thus attracted his attention for a whole day, acquiring such a clear idea of him that when he went home he would draw the head as well as if the man had been present. In this way many heads of men and women came to be drawn, and I have several such pen-and-ink drawings in my book, so often referred to. Among them is the head of Amerigo Vespucci,[21] a fine old man, drawn in carbon, and that of Scaramuccia, the captain of the gypsies, which afterwards belonged to Messer Donato Valdambrini of Arezzo, Canon of San Lorenzo, left to him by Giam-

20. The original is lost but there are several copies known, of which one of the best belonged once to Jacob Burckhardt and is now in the Basel Museum. Leonardo developed this composition, about ten years later, to a *St John* (plate 55).

21. In the Uffizi there is a portrait of Amerigo Vespucci as an old man. This portrait bears such resemblances to some of the heads in Leonardo's *Adoration of the Kings*, and even more to the Windsor drawing of *Judas* that the unknown

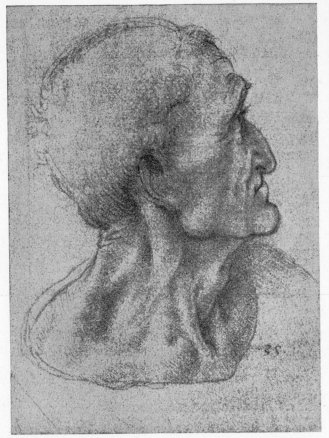

Leonardo: Study for the Judas in the Last Supper, red chalk on red paper, c. 1495. Windsor Castle, Royal Library (No. 12547).

Portrait of Amerigo Vespucci, by an unknown Florentine Painter, (copy after Leonardo?). Florence, Uffizi.

bullari. [22] He began a panel-picture of the Adoration of the Magi, containing many beautiful things, especially heads, which was in the house of Amerigo Benci, opposite the Loggia de' Peruzzi, but which was left unfinished like his other works. [23]

ON THE DEATH of Giovan Galeazzo, Duke of Milan, and the accession of Ludovico Sforza in the same year, 1494, [24] Leonardo was invited to Milan with great ceremony by the Duke to play the lute, in which that prince greatly delighted. Leonardo took his own instrument, made by himself in great part of silver, and shaped like a horse's head, a curious and novel idea to render the harmonies more loud and sonorous, so that he surpassed all the musicians who had assembled there. Besides this he was the best improviser of verse of his time. The Duke, captivated by Leonardo's conversation and genius,

painter of this portrait might be presumed to be familiar with Leonardo's charcoal-drawing. Amerigo Vespucci was born in 1454, and was therefore about the same age as Leonardo; he left Florence for Spain when he was forty, and never came back to Italy, as far as is known. Though I cannot discover where and when Leonardo could have drawn the likeness of the aged Amerigo Vespucci, the Leonardo-like portrait in the Uffizi would seem to corroborate Vasari's statement. (Cf. R. Langton Douglas, in *The Burlington Magazine*, February, 1944. But see also H. Brockhaus in *Forschungen über Florentiner Kunstwerke*, Leipzig, 1902, p. 83 f.)

22. There is a (much retouched) black chalk drawing at Christ Church, Oxford (B.B. 1050, fig. 536) of which Berenson thinks it might be the 'Scaramuccia', mentioned by Vasari.

23. Plates 49–53, and 103.

24. This date is certainly wrong. The Anonimo Gaddiano (see here, p. 30) says that Leonardo went to Milan when he was thirty years old; this means: in Spring, 1482. (See also Document I, p. 33.) In 1494, when Gian Galeazzo Sforza died, his uncle Ludovico had for already fourteen years been in full possession of all the power in Milan.

conceived an extraordinary affection for him. He begged him to paint an altar-piece of the Nativity, which was sent by the Duke to the Emperor.[25]

Leonardo then did a Last Supper for the Dominicans at Santa Maria delle Grazie in Milan, endowing the heads of the Apostles with such majesty and beauty that he left that of Christ unfinished, feeling that he could not give it that celestial divinity which it demanded.[26] This work left in such a condition has always been held in the greatest veneration by the Milanese and also by foreigners, as Leonardo has seized the moment when the Apostles are anxious to discover who would betray their Master. All their faces are expressive of love, fear, wrath or grief at not being able to grasp the meaning of Christ, in contrast to the obstinacy, hatred and treason of Judas, while the whole work, down to the smallest details, displays incredible diligence, even the texture of the tablecloth being clearly visible so that actual cambric would not look more real.

It is said that the Prior incessantly importuned Leonardo to finish the work, thinking it strange that the artist should pass half a day at a time lost in thought. He would have desired him never to lay down the brush, as if he were digging a garden. Seeing that his importunity produced no effect, he had recourse to the Duke, who felt compelled to send for Leonardo to inquire about the work, showing tactfully that he was driven to act by the importunity of the Prior. Leonardo, aware of the acuteness and discretion of the Duke, talked with him fully about the picture, a thing which he had never done with the Prior. He spoke freely of his art, and explained how men of genius really are doing most when they work least, as they are thinking out ideas and perfecting the conceptions, which they subsequently carry out with their hands. He added that there were still two heads to be done, that of Christ, which he would not look for on earth, and felt unable to conceive the beauty of the celestial grace that must have been incarnate in the divinity. The other head wanting for him to paint, was that of Judas, which also caused him thought, as he did not think he could express the face of a man who could resolve to betray his Master, the Creator of the world, after having received so many benefits. But he was willing in this case to seek no farther, and for lack of a better he would do the head of the importunate and tactless Prior. The Duke was wonderfully amused, and laughingly declared that he was quite right. Then the poor Prior, covered with confusion, went back to his garden and left Leonardo in peace, while the artist indeed finished his Judas, making him a veritable likeness of treason and cruelty. The head of Christ was left unfinished, as I have said. The nobility of this painting, in its composition and the care with which it was finished, induced the King of France to wish to take it home with him. Accordingly he employed architects to frame it in wood and iron, so that it might be transported in safety, without any regard for the cost, so great was his desire. But the King was thwarted by its being done on the wall, and it remained with the Milanese.

While engaged on the *Last Supper*, Leonardo painted on the end wall in the same refectory, where there is a *Passion* in the old style, the portrait of Duke Ludovico, with Maximilian, his eldest son, on the left; and on the right he did Duchess Beatrice with Francesco, her other son, both of whom afterwards became Dukes of Milan, the portraits being marvellous.[27]

---

25. See the note on plate 70.

26. Plates 71–75. See also plates 14–17; 89; and Appendix, plate IV.

27. The *Crucifixion* (which Vasari calls 'a Passion in the old style'), on the wall opposite Leonardo's *Last Supper*, is by Giovanni Donato Montorfano, dated 1495. The portraits

which Leonardo, according to Vasari, introduced into Montorfano's *Crucifixion*, are reproduced here as plate II in the Appendix. In 1945, when these photographs were taken, the figures were better visible than fifty years ago, as most of the retouchings have flaked off. Unfortunately, in the meantime a good deal of the original paint has also crumbled away, e.g. the whole face of Duke Ludovico.

While thus employed, Leonardo suggested that the Duke should set up a bronze horse of colossal size with the Duke upon it in memory of himself. But he began it on such a scale that it could never be done.[28] Such is the malice of man when stirred by envy that there are some who believe that Leonardo, as with so many of his works, began this with no intention of completing it, because its size was so great that extraordinary difficulties might be foreseen in having it cast all in one piece. And it is probable that many have formed this opinion from the result, since so many of his things have been left unfinished. However, we can readily believe that his great and extraordinary talents suffered a check from being too venturesome, and that the real cause was his endeavour to go on from excellence to excellence and from perfection to perfection. 'Thus the wish retarded the work', as our Petrarca says. In truth, those who have seen Leonardo's large clay model confess that they never beheld anything finer or more superb. It was preserved until the French came to Milan with King Louis of France, and broke it all to pieces. Thus a small wax model, considered perfect, was destroyed, as well as a book of the anatomy of horses, done by him.

He afterwards devoted even greater care to the study of the anatomy of men, aiding and being aided by Messer Marcantonio della Torre, a profound philosopher, who then professed at Padua and wrote upon the subject.[29] I have heard it said that he was one of the first who began to illustrate the science of medicine, by the learning of Galen, and to throw true light upon anatomy, up to that time involved in the thick darkness of ignorance. In this he was marvellously served by the genius, work and hands of Leonardo, who made a book about it with red chalk drawings outlined with the pen, in which he foreshortened and portrayed with the utmost diligence. He did the skeleton, adding all the nerves and muscles, the first attached to the bone, the others keeping it firm and the third moving, and in the various parts he wrote notes in curious characters, using his left hand, and writing from right to left, so that it cannot be read without practice, and only at a mirror.[30] A great part of the sheets of this anatomy is in the hands of Messer Francesco da Melzi, a nobleman of Milan, who was a lovely child in Leonardo's time, who was very fond of him, and being now a handsome and courteous old man, he treasures up these drawings with a portrait of Leonardo.[31] Whoever succeeds in reading

28. See plates 106 and VIII. The statue was not intended for Ludovico, but for his father, Francesco Sforza. The bronze horse is mentioned in Leonardo's famous letter to the Duke Ludovico, written probably in 1482: 'Again, the bronze horse may be taken in hand, which is to the immortal glory and eternal honour of the prince your father, of happy memory, and of the illustrious house of Sforza.' But the first sketches for this statue can be dated after 1485, and so it would seem that Leonardo did not begin this work immediately after his arrival in Milan.

The bronze horse was indeed planned to be of 'colossal size', about 24 feet high, twice as large as Verrocchio's *Colleoni*. According to Fra Luca Pacioli, Leonardo's friend, about 200,000 lb. of metal would have been required for the casting of the horse without the rider.

29. Marcantonio della Torre was professor of anatomy at the University of Padua and Pavia (1511); he died, when only thirty years old, in 1512. Leonardo's anatomical studies are in Windsor Castle (cf. Clark, pp. L–LIII. Richter II, 83). The earliest inventory of the Leonardo drawings in the Royal Collection confirms the collaboration therein of Marcantonio della Torre (Richter II, 399). The first scientific appreciation

of Leonardo's anatomical researches came from William Hunter, *Two introductory Lectures to his last course of anatomical lectures*, London, 1784. (See Prof. William Wright, in *Burlington Magazine*, May, 1919.) The best introduction to Leonardo's anatomical studies, is for English readers, J. Playfair McMurrich's *Leonardo da Vinci, the Anatomist*, Baltimore, 1930; and, for German readers, Sigrid Esche's *Leonardo: Das anatomische Werk*, Basel, 1953.

30. As Leonardo was left-handed (which is also confirmed by two of his contemporaries, Luca Pacioli and Sabba da Castiglione) he shaded his drawings from left to right.

31. Francesco Melzi, a nobleman of Milan, born 1493, died in Milan in 1570. He was a pupil and friend of Leonardo. He stayed with him in Rome (1513–16), and afterwards accompanied him to France. He was the executor of Leonardo's Will, and the Master bequeathed to him his library, his manuscripts, his instruments, some money, and even his clothes. In the Ambrosiana at Milan there are several drawings by Melzi; the 'Vertumnus and Pomona', in the Berlin Museum, the 'Columbine', in the Leningrad Hermitage, and some other paintings are attributed to him.

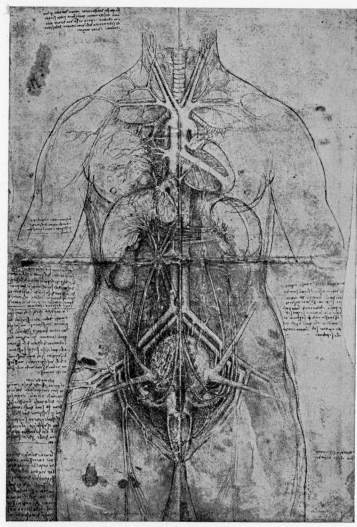

Leonardo: Anatomical study, pen and ink drawing over black chalk, c. 1513. Windsor Castle, Royal Library (No. 12281).

these notes of Leonardo will be amazed to find how well that divine spirit has reasoned of the arts, the muscles, the nerves and veins, with the greatest diligence in all things. N.N.,[32] a painter of Milan, also possesses some writings of Leonardo, written in the same way, which treat of painting and of the methods of design and colour. Not long ago he came to Florence to see me, wishing to have the work printed. He afterwards went to Rome to put it in hand, but I do not know with what result.[33]

To return to Leonardo's works. When Leonardo was at Milan the King of France came there and desired him to do something curious; accordingly he made a lion whose chest opened after he had walked a few steps, discovering himself to be full of lilies.[34] While at Milan Leonardo took Salai[35] of that city as his pupil. This was a graceful and beautiful youth with fine curly hair, in which Leonardo greatly delighted. He taught him many things in art, and some works which are attributed in Milan to Salai were retouched by Leonardo.[36]

HE RETURNED to Florence,[37] where he found that the Servite friars had allotted to Filippino the picture of the high altar of the Annunziata. At this Leonardo declared that he should like to have done

32. Vasari does not give the owner's name. As the manuscript is not mentioned at all in the first edition of his *Vite*, he can only have seen it between 1551 and 1567. (The Milanese painter N.N. was either Lomazzo, or Aurelio Luini.)

33. The first printed edition was published in 1651 by Raphael du Fresne in Paris. The first English translation was issued (anonymously) in 1721, London. But the *Trattato della Pittura* is a mere compilation by some disciple. For Leonardo's Manuscripts, see Bibliography, p. 40.

34. An automaton, such as had been constructed ever since ancient times. Vasari's story is confirmed by Lomazzo (*Trattato dell'arte*, Milan, 1585, p. 106; and *Idea del tempio*, Milan, 1590, p. 17). Lomazzo states that he heard from Francesco Melzi that this lion was made for Francis the First. Similar sketches may be found on a sheet (fol. 179 recto) of the *Codice Atlantico* (published by Müller-Walde, *Prussian*

Jahrbuch, 1898, p. 233). Lomazzo was also told that Leonardo constructed artificial birds which flew through the air. (Similar automatons were made by the Emperor Charles the Fifth on his retirement to a monastery.)

35. Giacomo Salai came to live with Leonardo as a boy of ten, on the 22nd July, 1490. He was obviously a child of bad character—Leonardo called him 'thief, liar, glutton'. But the Master kept him for twenty-five years, gave him expensive presents, including a cloak of silver brocade, trimmed with green velvet, and a pair of rose-coloured tights; nor did he forget him in his Will. Emil Möller (*Salai und Leonardo*, in the *Vienna Jahrbuch*, NF II, 1928, p. 139 et seq.) attributed a number of beautiful paintings to Salai.

36. A letter from the White Friar, Pietro da Novellara, to Isabella d'Este, 1501, states that Leonardo corrected and retouched the paintings of his pupils.

37. April 1500.

a similar thing. Filippino heard this, and being very courteous, he withdrew. The friars, wishing Leonardo to paint it, brought him to their house, paying all his expenses and those of his household. He kept them like this for a long time, but never began anything. At length he drew a cartoon of the Virgin and St Anne with a Christ, which not only filled every artist with wonder, but, when it was finished and set up in the room, men and women, young and old, flocked to see it for two days, as if it had been a festival, and they marvelled exceedingly.[38] The face of the Virgin displays all the simplicity and beauty which can shed grace on the Mother of God, showing the modesty and humility of a Virgin contentedly happy in seeing the beauty of her Son, whom she tenderly holds in her lap. As she regards Him, the little St John at her feet caresses a lamb, while St Anne smiles in her great joy at seeing her earthly progeny become divine, a conception worthy of the great intellect and genius of Leonardo. This cartoon, as will be said below, afterwards went to France.[39] He drew Ginevra, the daughter of Amerigo Benci, a beautiful portrait,[40] and then abandoned the work of the friars, who recalled Filippino, though he was prevented from finishing it by death.[41]

For Francesco del Giocondo Leonardo undertook the portrait of Mona Lisa, his wife, and left it incomplete after working at it for four years.[42] This work is now in the possession of Francis, King of France, at Fontainebleau. This head is an extraordinary example of how art can imitate Nature, because here we have all the details painted with great subtlety. The eyes possess that moist lustre which is constantly seen in life, and about them are those livid reds and hair which cannot be rendered without the utmost delicacy. The brows could not be more natural for the way in which the hairs issue from the skin, here thick and there scanty, following the pores of the skin. The nose possesses the fine nostrils, rosy and tender, as seen in life. The opening of the mouth, with its red lips, and the scarlet cheeks seem not colour but living flesh. To look closely at her throat you might imagine that the pulse was beating. Indeed, we may say that this was painted in a manner to cause the boldest artists to despair. Mona Lisa was very beautiful, and while Leonardo was drawing her portrait he engaged people to play and sing, and jesters to keep her merry, and remove that melancholy which painting usually gives to portraits. This figure of Leonardo's has such a pleasant smile that it seemed rather divine than human, and was considered marvellous, an exact copy of life.

The fame of this divine artist grew to such a pitch by the excellence of his works that all who delighted in the arts and the whole city wished him to leave some memorial, and they endeavoured to think of some noteworthy decorative work through which the State might be adorned and honoured by the genius, grace and judgment characteristic of his work. The great hall of the council was being rebuilt under the direction of Giuliano da San Gallo, Simone Pollaiuolo called Il Cronaca, Michelangelo Buonarroti and Baccio d'Agnolo, by the judgment and advice of the Gonfaloniere,[43] and leading

38. See William R. Valentiner, *Über zwei Kompositionen Leonardos*, in the *Prussian Jahrbuch*, vol. 56, 1935, p. 213 f. This version of the St Anne was not carried beyond the stage of a cartoon (see note on plate 54). In 1503 the commission was transferred to Filippino Lippi, who painted a *Crucifixion* for the High-altar of S. Annunziata (now Uffizi, No. 8370), but died before he had finished it. Filippino's *Crucifixion* was finished by Perugino in 1505.

39. Suida, *Leonardo und sein Kreis*, p. 130. See Document XI.

40. Plates 23 and 88.

41. See footnote 38.

42. Plates 28-29.

43. Gonfaloniere di Giustizia, the 'standard-bearer of justice', the highest Florentine magistrate. In the Life of Cronaca Vasari says: 'At the same time it was proposed to make the great hall of the Signoria at Florence for the council of Fra Girolamo Savonarola, the famous preacher [July, 1495]. Upon this a consultation was held with Leonardo da Vinci, Michelangelo Buonarroti, then a youth, Giuliano da San Gallo, Baccio d'Agnolo, and Simone Pollaiuolo, called Il Cronaca. . . . After many discussions it was agreed that the hall should be made as it always stood until its restoration in our own day.' If this statement of Vasari's is correct, Leonardo was for some time in Florence before he started the work on the Last Supper in Milan.

citizens, as will be related at greater length in another place, and being finished with great speed, it was ordained by public decree that Leonardo should be employed to paint some fine work. Thus the hall was allotted to him by Piero Soderini, then Gonfaloniere of Justice. Leonardo began by drawing a cartoon at the hall of the Pope,[44] a place in Santa Maria Novella, containing the story of Niccolò Piccinino, captain of Duke Filippo of Milan.[45] Here he designed a group of horsemen fighting for a standard, a masterly work on account of his treatment of the fight, displaying the wrath, anger and vindictiveness of men and horses; two of the latter, with their front legs involved, are waging war with their teeth no less fiercely than their riders are fighting for the standard. One soldier, putting his horse to the gallop, has turned round and grasping the staff of the standard, is endeavouring by main force to wrench it from the hands of four others, while two are defending it, trying to cut the staff with their swords; an old soldier in a red cap has a hand on the staff, as he cries out, and holds a scimitar in the other and threatens to cut off both hands of the two, who are grinding their teeth and making every effort to defend their banner. On the ground, between the legs of the horses, are two fore-shortened figures who are fighting together, while a soldier lying prone has another over him who is raising his arm as high as he can to run his dagger with his utmost strength into his adversary's throat; the latter, whose legs and arms are helpless, does what he can to escape death. The manifold designs Leonardo made for the costumes of his soldiers defy description, not to speak of the scimitars and other ornaments, and his incredible mastery of form and line in dealing with horses, which he made better than any other master, with their powerful muscles and graceful beauty. It is said that for designing the cartoon he made an ingenious scaffolding which rose higher when pressed together and broadened out when lowered. Thinking that he could paint on the wall in oils, he made a composition so thick for laying on the wall that when he continued his painting it began to run and spoil what had been begun, so that in a short time he was forced to abandon it.[46]

Leonardo had a high spirit and was most generous in every action. It is said that when he went to the bank for the monthly provision that he used to receive from Piero Soderini, the cashier wanted to give him some rolls of farthings, but he would not take them, saying that he was not a painter for farthings. Learning that Piero Soderini accused him of deceiving him and that murmurs rose against him, Leonardo with the help of his friends collected the money and took it back, but Piero would not accept it.

He went to Rome[47] with Duke Giuliano de' Medici on the election of Leo X, who studied philosophy and especially alchemy. On the way he made a paste with wax and constructed hollow animals which flew in the air when blown up, but fell when the wind ceased. On a curious lizard found by the vine-dresser of Belvedere he fastened scales taken from other lizards, dipped in quicksilver, which trembled as it moved, and after giving it eyes, a horn and a beard, he tamed it and kept it in a box. All the friends to whom he showed it ran away terrified. He would often dry and clean the guts of a bullock and make them so small that they might be held in the palm of the hand. In another room he kept a pair of smith's bellows, and with these he would blow out one of the guts until it filled the room, which was a large one, forcing anyone there to take refuge in a corner. The fact that it

44. Thus called because this part of the Convent was the abode of different Popes during the 15th and 16th centuries.

45. The Battle of Anghiari, 29th June, 1440; a victory of the Florentines over a Milanese army. See plates 108–110.

46. The original cartoon, on which Leonardo worked from October 1503 till February 1505, is lost, as also is the mural which had to give way to one of Vasari's murals when the room was redecorated from 1558 onward.

47. 24th September, 1513; in August 1516 he was still there.

had occupied such a little space at first only added to the wonder. He perpetrated many such follies, studied mirrors and made curious experiments to find oil for painting and varnish to preserve the work done.

At this time he did a small picture for Messer Baldassare Turini of Pescia, the Datary of Pope Leo, of the Virgin and Child, with infinite diligence and art. [48] But today it is much spoiled either by neglect or because of his numerous fanciful mixtures of ground and colouring. In another little picture he represented a boy, marvellously beautiful and graceful, both works being now at Pescia in the possession of Messer Giulio Turini. [49]

It is said that, on being commissioned by the Pope to do a work, he straightway began to distil oil and herbs to make the varnish, which induced Pope Leo to say: 'This man will never do anything, for he begins to think of the end before the beginning!'

There was no love lost between Leonardo and Michelangelo Buonarroti, so that the latter left Florence owing to their rivalry, Duke Giuliano excusing him by saying that he was summoned by the Pope to do the façade of San Lorenzo. [50] When Leonardo heard this, he left for France, where the king had heard of his works and wanted him to do the cartoon of St Anne in colours. [51] But Leonardo, as was his wont, gave him nothing but words for a long time. At length, having become old, he lay sick for many months, and seeing himself near death, he desired to occupy himself with the truths of the Catholic Faith and the holy Christian religion. Then, having confessed and shown his penitence with much lamentation, he devoutly took the Sacrament, leaving his bed, supported by his friends and servants, as he could not stand. The king arriving, for he would often pay him friendly visits, he sat up in bed from respect, and related the circumstances of his sickness, showing how greatly he had offended God and man in not having worked in his art as he ought. He was then seized with a paroxysm, the harbinger of death, so that the king rose and took his head to assist him and show him favour as well as to alleviate the pain. Leonardo's divine spirit, then recognizing that he could not enjoy a greater honour, expired in the king's arms, at the age of seventy-five. [52]

The loss of Leonardo caused exceptional grief to those who had known him, because there never was a man who did so much honour to painting. By the splendour of his magnificent countenance he comforted every sad soul, and his eloquence could turn men to either side of a question. His personal strength was prodigious, and with his right hand he could bend the clapper of a knocker or a horseshoe as if they had been of lead. His liberality warmed the hearts of all his friends, both rich and poor, if they possessed talent and ability. His presence adorned and honoured the most wretched and bare apartment. Thus Florence received a great gift in the birth of Leonardo, and its loss in his death was immeasurable.

To the art of painting in oil he added a certain mode of deepening the shadows, by which the moderns have imparted great vigour and relief to their figures. He proved his powers in statuary in three figures in bronze over the door of San Giovanni on the north side. They were executed by

48. Lost.

49. Probably the Infant Jesus. The picture is lost; Rio thought that it was burnt in Whitehall. (See also the note on plate 7, p. 152.)

50. Michelangelo worked on the façade of San Lorenzo from 1516 to 1520 in Florence and made during this period only occasional visits to Rome. By the end of 1516, or perhaps in Spring 1517, Leonardo left for France.

51. Plate 68. The *St Anne* was painted during the second stay in Milan, c. 1508–10.

52. Leonardo died on May 2nd, 1519, when sixty-seven years old. A letter from Francesco Melzi from Amboise, dated June 1st, 1519, to Leonardo's brothers, does not mention the King, who, on the day of Leonardo's death, was, in fact, not in Amboise, but with the Court at St. Germain-en-Laye. (Document XVII.)

Giovan Francesco Rustici, but under Leonardo's direction, and are the finest casts for design and general perfection that have as yet been seen in modern times.[53]

To Leonardo we owe a greater perfection in the anatomy of the horse, and the anatomy of man. Thus, by his many surpassing gifts, although he laboured far more by words than by his deeds, his name and fame will never be extinguished.[54]

Giovan Antonio Boltraffio of Milan was a pupil of Leonardo, and a very skilful and intelligent man, who in 1500 painted a panel in oils in the church of the Misericordia, outside Bologna, with the Virgin and Child, St John the Baptist, and a nude St Sebastian, including a portrait of the donor kneeling.[55] To this fine work he signed his name, adding that he was a pupil of Leonardo. He did other works at Milan and elsewhere, but the one I have just referred to is the best. Marco Uggioni,[56] another pupil, painted the Death of the Virgin and the Marriage of Cana in Galilee in Santa Maria della Pace.[57]

---

53. Plate v in the Appendix, and the note to this plate.

54. Here follows in the original text an epigram by Messer Giovan Battista Strozzi in praise of Leonardo: '*Vince costo pur solo/Tutti altri, vince Fidia, vince Apelle/E tutto il lor vittorioso stuolo.*' This play upon words – *vincere*, to vanquish, and *Vinci* – cannot be translated into English. The meaning of the epigram is roughly: 'Single-handed he vanquished all the others, Phidias, Apelles, and their whole victorious troop.'

55. Born 1467, died 1516. The picture, mentioned by Vasari, is now in the Louvre, No. 1169; painted in 1500, for the Casio family. Two kneeling donors, Giacomo and Giro-lamo Casio, are represented in this picture. According to an old tradition (Baldinucci), Leonardo himself helped with the painting. In the National Gallery, London, there are a *Profile of a Man* and a *Madonna* by Boltraffio's hand.

56. Marco d'Oggiono (or De Uglono), born about 1477 at Oggiono near Milan; worked in Leonardo's workshop from about 1490 to 1499; died in Milan about 1530. The copy he made of Leonardo's 'Last Supper', now at The Royal Academy, London, is well known. The National Gallery, London (No. 1149) owns one of his Madonnas.
(See W. Suida, Marco d'Oggiono, in *Raccolta Vinciana*, 1939, pp. 127–155.)

57. The two pictures from Santa Maria della Pace in Milan are now in the Brera, Milan; Nos. 79 and 81.

Portrait of the Florentine poet *Bernardo Bellinzone*, engaged at the Court of
Ludovico Sforza. Woodcut, based (according to Amoretti and Kristeller)
on a drawing by Leonardo. From Bellinzone's *Rime*, Milan 1493.

ADDITIONAL REFERENCES CONCERNING
LEONARDO DA VINCI
TAKEN FROM SIX OTHER 'VITE' BY VASARI · 1568

In the *'Life of Giorgione'*:

Having seen and greatly admired some things of Leonardo, richly toned and exceedingly dark, as has been said, Giorgione made them his model, and imitated them carefully in painting in oil.[58]

58. *'Exceedingly dark' connects Giorgione's first style with Leonardo's 'chiaroscuro', mentioned in his Life by Vasari (p. 15). Leonardo passed through Venice in 1500 and perhaps also in 1503 and 1506. 'But in 1507', says Vasari in the Life of Titian, 'arose Giorgione, who began to give his works more tone and relief, with better style'. How far the young Giorgione made him his model can be seen from his 'Christ carrying the Cross' (cf. note on plate 98), but still more from his 'Judith' in the Hermitage, which seems to me more Leonardesque than all the copies of the standing 'Leda' attributed to the School of Leonardo. Leonardo's knot pattern is used as an ornament on the dress of the Brocardo portrait by Giorgione in the Budapest Museum.*

In the *'Life of Andrea del Verrocchio'*:

There are some of Andrea's drawings in our possession . . . among them being some female heads so beautiful and with such charming hair that Leonardo was always imitating them. [See also the illustration on p. 25.]
We have besides two [drawings of] horses, squared and measured proportions, by which method they can be increased to a large scale without error.[59]

59. *Some of Verrocchio's drawings are sometimes attributed to Leonardo; e.g. the famous silverpoint drawing in Dresden, connected with the Pistoia altar-piece (reproduced, Berenson, No. 672, Fig. 139); a Madonna head in Paris (repr. Suida, plate 4); and others. One of Verrocchio's drawings of a horse 'with measures and proportions' is in the Metropolitan Museum, New York (at one time attributed to Leonardo by Sirén).*

In the *'Life of Piero di Cosimo'*:

He practised painting in oil after seeing some things by Leonardo toned and finished with the extreme diligence characteristic of that Master when he wished to display his art. This method pleased Piero, and he strove to imitate it, though he was a long way behind Leonardo.[60]

60. *Piero di Cosimo borrowed from Leonardo's Madonna drawings. Suida contends that his painting 'Perseus and Andromeda' in the Florence Uffizi (No. 1536) is taken from a drawing by Leonardo, or even executed with his help. He was not the first to express this opinion. In the inventory of the Uffizi Gallery, made in 1580, the picture is mentioned as drawn by Leonardo and coloured by Piero di Cosimo. Morelli (Galleries in Rome, English ed., 1892, p. 120) said 'Several of the heads have not*

only Leonardo's sfumato, but recall the Gioconda in expression'. And Maud Cruttwell (A Guide to the Paintings in the Florentine Galleries, 1907, p. 98): 'The female crouched in the foreground with a strange-shaped musical instrument is worthy of Leonardo, who it is not impossible may have designed it.'

In the Chapter on *'Lombard Artists'*:

In the Mint at Milan there is a copy of a portrait of a smiling woman by Leonardo done by Fra Girolamo [Monsignori] and of a young St John the Baptist, very well imitated.[61]

61. *This passage from Vasari shows that even in the middle of the 16th century it was not easy to distinguish Leonardo's work from imitations.*

In the *'Life of Raphael'*:

In his childhood Raphael imitated the style of Pietro Perugino, his master, improving it greatly in design, colouring and invention. But in riper years he perceived that this was too far from the truth. For he saw the works of Leonardo da Vinci, who had no equal in the expression which he gave to his heads of women and children, while in the grace and movement of his figures he surpassed all other artists; this filled Raphael with wonder and amazement. As Leonardo's style pleased him more than any he had ever seen, he set to work to study it, and gradually and painfully abandoning the manner of Pietro, he sought as far as possible to imitate Leonardo; and, though some consider him superior in sweetness, and in a certain natural facility, yet he never excelled that wonderful ground-work of ideas and that grandeur of art, in which few have equalled Leonardo. Raphael, however, approached him more closely than any other painter, especially in grace of colouring.[62]

62. *How much Raphael borrowed from Leonardo cannot be told in a single note. He was indebted to Leonardo's Anghiari cartoon, his standing Leda with the Swan, and his Mona Lisa. From a drawing of the Mona Lisa, Raphael painted his portrait of Maddalena Doni. Raphael's 'Family with the Lamb' is copied freely from Leonardo's first St Anne cartoon; his Madonna with the Flower, his Esterházy Madonna, his Madonna Alba, in fact most of his Madonna paintings are either directly derived from drawings by Leonardo, or are variations of them. It may sound paradoxical, but it seems that Leonardo had only two true disciples: Raphael and Dürer.*

Verrocchio: *Marble bust of a Lady holding primulas.* About 1475–78. (By Mackowsky, Suida, and others, attributed to Leonardo.)
Florence, Bargello.

(25)

Leonardo: *Madonna Benois*. About 1478–80. (At one time attributed to Lorenzo di Credi, or Sogliani.)
Leningrad, Hermitage. (Cf. pl. 57.)

Verrocchio and Lorenzo di Credi: *The Pistoia Altar-piece* (*'Madonna di Piazza'*). 1475–1485. Pistoia, Cathedral.

In the '*Life of Lorenzo di Credi*':
His ambition rising, Lorenzo went to Andrea del Verrocchio, whose whim was then painting. Under this master he had as friends and companions, although rivals, Pietro Perugino and Leonardo da Vinci, both diligently studying painting. Leonardo's style greatly delighted Lorenzo, who succeeded better than any others in imitating his polish and finish.

Lorenzo's first work was a circular painting (tondo) of a Madonna sent to the King of Spain, the design being taken from one of Andrea del Verrocchio's. He then did a far better picture, copied from one by Leonardo da Vinci, and also sent to Spain. It could not be distinguished from the original.[63]

63. *Some works of Lorenzo di Credi were sometimes ascribed to Leonardo, and vice versa. Thus, for instance, the Liechtenstein portrait (plate 23), the Benois Madonna (plate 57), the Uffizi Annunciation (plate 59) were once attributed to Credi. On the other hand, the predella of the Pistoia altar-piece, the Louvre Annunciation, and 'San Donato of Arezzo and the Tax Collector' in the Worcester Art Museum, Mass., were thought to be by Leonardo (Appendix, plate I). The Pistoia altar-piece was produced in Verrocchio's workshop, 1475–1485; it was begun by the Master himself but finished by Credi. Leonardo probably had a share in it. About eight years older than Credi, Leonardo was not only his co-pupil in Verrocchio's workshop but his teacher as well.*

A NOTE ON
THE EARLIEST BIOGRAPHIES OF LEONARDO DA VINCI
PAOLO GIOVIO – ANONIMO GADDIANO – LIBRO DI ANTONIO BILLI –
AND SABBA DA CASTIGLIONE'S RICORDI

THE following two short accounts cannot compare in literary value with Vasari's pages on Leonardo; but they are earlier.

Paolo Giovio was born in 1483 at Como, not far from Milan, where at that time Leonardo lived; he studied at Padua and then practised surgery at Milan. In 1517 he went to Rome; but while doctor to Pope Leo X, he spent most of his time reading the classics and preparing his *Historia sui temporis* in forty-five parts (which was printed, 1548–52, in two folio volumes at Florence). After Giovio had lost all his books and papers during the sack of Rome in 1527, Pope Clement VII made him bishop of Nocera. He took great interest in the art of portraiture, and collected a large number of portraits of famous men and women. The 'Museum Jovianum' in Giovio's villa on the Lake of Como was a kind of National Portrait Gallery; there were so many portraits that it took Cristoforo dell' Altissimo twelve years to paint a selection of 240 copies for Grand Duke Cosimo I. Giovio died at Florence in 1552.

Giovio's three eulogies on famous men and women, of which the short Leonardo biography forms a part of the unfinished third eulogy, were written on the island of Ischia, where the author had retired for a short time after the sack of Rome in 1527. (Paolo Giovio, *De viris illustribus*, in Tiraboschi's *Storia della letteratura italiana*, Modena, 1781, vol. IX, p. 290 f.)

The translation from the Latin of Giovio's Leonardo biography is by J. P. Richter and was first printed in his edition of *The Literary Works of Leonardo da Vinci*, vol. I, p. 3, London, 1939. (I have added a few footnotes.)

The second biography is about fifteen years later and by an anonymous writer, called *Anonimo Gaddiano*, or *Magliabecchiano*. (The manuscript, now in the Biblioteca Nazionale at Florence, belonged before to the Biblioteca Gaddiana, and after that to the Biblioteca Magliabecchiana.) The English translation of this biography is by Kate T. Steinitz and Ebria Feinblatt, and was first published in the Leonardo Exhibition Catalogue of the Los Angeles County Museum, 1949. (The footnotes are my own.)

The Anonimo made use of a page on Leonardo in the 'Book of Antonio Billi', which was written in about 1518. Those thirty lines contain only one point of interest, namely the statement that Leonardo was cheated over the linseed oil which he used in painting the *Anghiari Battle*, and that this was reponsible for the fast decay of the mural. ('*Dettesi la colpa, che lui fu ingannato nello olio del seme del lino, che gli fu falsato.*') Billi also says: 'Not many things did Leonardo in colour, because never and with nothing, not even the most beautiful he did, he was satisfied: and for this reason there are so very few paintings by him, as his great knowledge about errors in work prohibited him from working.' As to the rest, Billi gives a short list of Leonardo's works in the following order: The portrait of Ginevra de' Benci – A panel of the Madonna – A St John – An altar-piece which Ludovico Moro sent to the German Emperor – The Last Supper – The clay model of the huge Equestrian Monument for Francesco Sforza – A large number of marvellous drawings: a Saint Anne, that went to France; and the cartoon of the Anghiari Battle. As the author of the 'Book of Antonio Billi' mentions the *St Anne* amongst the drawings, he apparently means a cartoon, and not a painting (see also p. 31).

These three short biographies are earlier than Vasari's *Vita di Leonardo*; so are also the *Ricordi* by Sabba da Castiglione (Bologna 1546). Castiglione wrote as an old man who had known Leonardo; he mentions *The Last Supper*, and the Sforza monument, on which, he says, Leonardo worked for sixteen years; he also describes how the model was destroyed; he states that Leonardo was left-handed; and he thinks that Leonardo finished so very few works because he devoted most of his time to Architecture, Geometry and Anatomy.

I

THE LIFE OF LEONARDO DA VINCI
BY PAOLO GIOVIO

Leonardo, born at Vinci, an insignificant hamlet in Tuscany, has added great lustre to the art of painting. He established that all proper practice of this art should be preceded by a training in the sciences and the liberal arts which he regarded as indispensable and subordinate to painting. He placed modelling as a means of rendering figures in relief on a flat surface before other processes done with the brush. The science of optics was to him of paramount importance and on it he founded the principles of the distribution of light and shade down to the most minute details. In order that he might be able to paint the various joints and muscles as they bend and stretch according to the laws of nature, he dissected in medical schools the corpses of criminals, indifferent to this inhuman and nauseating work. He then tabulated with extreme accuracy all the different parts down to the smallest veins and the composition of the bones, in order that this work on which he had spent so many years should be published from copper engravings for the benefit of art. But while he was thus spending his time in the close research of subordinate branches of his art he carried only very few works to completion; for owing to his masterly facility and the fastidiousness of his nature, he discarded works he had already begun. However, the wall painting at Milan of Christ at Supper with His Disciples is greatly admired. [1] It is said that when King Louis saw it he coveted it so much that he inquired anxiously from those standing around him whether it could be detached from the wall and transported forthwith to France, although this would have destroyed the famous refectory. There is also the picture of the infant Christ playing with His mother, the Virgin, and His grandmother, Anne, which King Francis of France bought and placed in his chapel. [2] Moreover, there remains the painting of the battle and victory over the Pisans [3] in the Council Chamber at Florence which was extraordinarily magnificent but came to an untimely end owing to the defective plaster which persistently rejected the colors ground in walnut oil. It seems as if the very natural regret caused by this unexpected injury and interruption of the work was instrumental in making it famous. For Lodovico Sforza he made also a clay model of a colossal horse to be cast in bronze, on which was to be seated the figure of the famous condottiere Francesco, Lodovico's father. [4] The vehement life-like action of this horse as if panting is amazing, not less so the sculptor's skill and his consummate knowledge of nature. His charm of disposition, his brilliancy and generosity were not less than the beauty of his appearance. His genius for invention was astounding, and he was the arbiter of all questions relating to beauty and elegance, especially in pageantry. He sang beautifully to his own accompaniment on the lyre to the delight of the entire court. He died in France at the age of sixty-seven [5] to the grief of his friends, which loss was all the greater for among the great crowd of young men who contributed to the success of his studio he left no disciple of outstanding fame.

1. Plate 73.

2. Plate 68.

3. Plate 108 (a copy of the lost cartoon). Leonardo's *Battle of Anghiari* represented a victory of the Florentines over the Milanese, and not, as Giovio says, over the Pisans. (It was Michelangelo's *Battle of Cascina* that gave a scene from the Pisan war.)

4. See note on plate 106.

5. This is correct. The Anonimo Gaddiano and Vasari are giving wrongly Leonardo's age at the time of his death.

LEONARDO DA VINCI
BY THE ANONIMO GADDIANO
ALSO CALLED ANONIMO MAGLIABECCHIANO

A Florentine citizen who, although he was the illegitimate son of Ser Piero da Vinci, was born of good blood on his mother's side. He was so unusual and many-sided that nature seemed to have produced a miracle in him, not only in the beauty of his person, but in the many gifts with which she endowed him and which he fully mastered. Greatly talented in mathematics, he was no less so in the science of perspective, while in the field of sculpture and design he far surpassed all others. He made many excellent inventions, but because it was hard for him to be satisfied with his work we find but few paintings from his hand. An eloquent speaker, he was an exquisite musician on the lyre and taught the singer Atalante Migliorotti. [6] He was delightfully inventive, and was most skillful in lifting weights, in building waterworks and other imaginative constructions, nor did his mind ever come to rest, but dwelt always with ingenuity on the creation of new inventions.

As a young man he was with Lorenzo de' Medici the Magnificent, and with his support he worked in the gardens of his palace in San Marco in Florence. When he was thirty years of age it is said that the Magnificent sent him to the Duke of Milan to present, with Atalante Migliorotti, the gift of a lyre, which the latter could play with rare execution. Later he returned to Florence where he remained for some time, but then, either because of some kind of indignation or other causes, while working in the hall of the Council of the Signoria, [7] he left and went back to Milan where he served the Duke for a few years. Afterwards he was with Cesare Borgia, the Duke Valentino, and then also in France in several places, before returning to Milan. [8] While preparing to cast his equestrian monument in bronze a revolution in the state brought him back to Florence, where for six months he stayed in the house of Giovanni Francesco Rustici, sculptor of the via Martelli. [9] Once more he returned to Milan, and then finally went to France in the service of the king, Francis I. He took with him enough of his drawings, leaving some again in the Hospital of Santa Maria Nuova, Florence, together with other household goods, and the greater part of a cartoon in the Council Hall, of which the design of a group of horses can be seen today in the Palace. [10] He died near Amboise, a French city, at the age of seventy-two, [11] in a place called Cloux, which he had made his home. He left in his testament everything to Messer Francesco da Melzi, a nobleman of Milan, all his money and clothes, books, writings, drawings, instruments, and his treatises on painting, art and his industriousness, and whatever else could be found, and made him executor of his will. [12] To his servant Battista Villani he left half of his garden on the outskirts of Milan, and the other half to Salai, his pupil. He left four hundred ducats to his brothers, depositing the sum in the Hospital of Santa Maria Nuova in Florence, but after his death only three hundred ducats were found.

6. Atalante was famous as a maker of musical instruments, and also as an actor and a singing master. In 1490 he became the leading singer of the Ducal Opera House at Mantua. In 1513 he was in Rome where Leonardo must have met him again.

7. Working on the *Battle of Anghiari*, 1503–06.

8. Leonardo was in the service of Cesare Borgia in 1502–03, for about six months. He returned to Milan in 1506, where he served the King of France and his governor; a visit to France in the period 1503–06 is not known and is highly improbable.

9. See note on plate VI.

10. See note on plate 108.

11. Should read *sixty-seven*.

12. For the complete text of Leonardo's last Will see Richter II, § 1566.

Among his pupils were Salai of Milan, Zoroastro of Peretola, Riccio Fioerntino of the Porta al Croce, Ferrando the Spaniard, who worked with him in the Hall of the Signoria Palace.[13]

In Florence he painted the portrait of Ginevra d'Amerigho Benci from nature, a work which was so finished that it seemed not a portrait but Ginevra herself.[14]

He made a panel of Our Lady, a most excellent work.

He also painted a Saint John.[15]

And again a Leda.[16] He painted Adam and Eve in water colour, today in the house of Messer Ottaviano de' Medici.

He made the portrait from nature of Piero Francesco del Giocondo.[17]

He painted . . . a head of Medusa with a wonderful and unique collection of serpents; today it is in the chamber of the most Illustrious and Excellent Signor Duke Cosimo de' Medici.

He was commissioned to paint in the great Council Hall of the Palace in Florence a cartoon of the battle of Florentines, during the time at Anghiari when they attacked Niccholo Piccin[in]o, the captain of Duke Filippo of Milan, and he began the work in that place as can be seen there today; and with varnish. . . .

He undertook to paint a panel in the same Palace, which was later finished after his design by Filippo di Fra Filippo.[18]

He painted an altar panel for Signor (the Duke) Lodovico of Milan, which those who have seen it declare to be the most beautiful and unusual work to be found in painting, and which the afore-mentioned lord sent . . . to the Emperor.

He also painted in Milan a Last Supper, a most excellent work.[19]

Again in Milan he likewise made a horse of immense grandeur, bearing upon it the Duke Francesco Sforza, a most beautiful work which was to be cast in bronze, a feat universally judged impossible, especially since he said he desired to cast it all in one piece; this work was never realized.[20]

He made innumerable drawings, all marvellous things, and among them a Madonna and a Saint Anne,[21] which went to France, and anatomical studies which he drew in the Hospital of Santa Maria Nuova in Florence.

13. About Ferrando de Llanos see Elizabeth du Gué Trapier, *Luis Morales and the Leonardesque influences in Spain*, New York, 1953.

14. See note on plate 23.

15. This St John and the panel of Our Lady, both probably painted in Florence, are also mentioned in the *Libro di Antonio Billi* (see p. 28). The *St John* was perhaps a version of the *Angel of the Annunciation*, illustrated here on p. 15.

16. The manuscript reads here, according to Carl Frey, p. 369: '*Et anchora [una Leda] dipinse Adamo et Eva d'aquarello.*' The two words put here in square brackets are crossed out in the manuscript. – See plate 37.

17. Carl Frey, p. 372, suspects here a slip of the pen and suggests: '*Ritrasse dal naturale moglie di Francesco del Giocondo*'. This would mean the portrait of Mona Lisa (plate 28).

18. Contract, dated 1478, for the Chapel of San Bernardino in the Palazzo Vecchio. Valentiner accepted the statement of the Anonimo as correct and identified the San Bernardino altar-piece with Filippino Lippi's picture of a Madonna with four saints, dated February 20th, 1485 (now Uffizi No. 1568). – Another altar-piece was ordered first from Leonardo, and then from Filippino Lippi, by the monks of San Donato a Scopeto outside Florence. Leonardo received his commission in 1481 and left the picture unfinished (plate 49). Fifteen years later the order was transferred to Filippino Lippi (*Adoration of the Kings*, dated 1496, now Uffizi No. 1257). – There was a third encounter of the two artists, of which we know through Vasari (see footnote 38 on p. 20).

19. Plate 73.

20. See note on plate 111.

21. Probably the cartoon of 1501; see also note on plate 54.

The following supplement to the biography is introduced by the words Dal Gav. *This is supposed to refer to Giovanni di Gavina, a Florentine painter and friend of Leonardo, who related it to the Anonimo Gaddiano. Carl Frey and J. Wilde, however, read* Dal Cav. *and explain it as Cavaliere Bandinelli.*

Leonardo da Vinci was a contemporary of Michelangelo, and from Pliny he took the recipe for the pigments with which he painted, but without fully understanding it. The first time he demonstrated it upon a wall in the Hall of the Pope, where he was working, he placed a great fire of burning coals in front of it, whereby through the heat the material would be dried and fixed. After that, desiring to put the work in the Hall (of the Council), it turned out that the fire dried and joined the lower part of the fresco, but was unable to reach the upper section, due to the great distance, and this part did not come together and the colours ran.

Beautiful in person and aspect, Leonardo was well-proportioned and graceful. He wore a rose-coloured cloak, which came only to his knees, although at the time long vestments were the custom. His beard came to the middle of his breast and was well-dressed and curled.

Leonardo, in the company of Giovanni di Gavina of Santa Trinita, passed the benches of the Palazzo Spini one day, where a group of gentlemen were disputing over a passage in Dante. They appealed to Leonardo to explain the lines to them. Exactly at this moment Michelangelo passed by and Leonardo replied to the questioners, 'Michelangelo will explain it to you'. Michelangelo responded with anger, since it seemed to him that Leonardo was making mock of him, 'You made a design for a horse to be cast in bronze, and, unable to cast it, have in your shame abandoned it'. And saying this, he turned his heels to them and left the street. And Leonardo remained at these words and blushed.

And to annoy Leonardo, Michelangelo called after him: 'And those Milanese idiots did believe in you?'

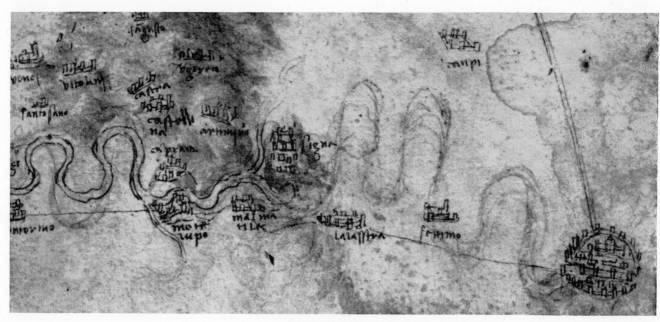

The country between Vinci and Florence. Pen and ink drawing by Leonardo da Vinci, c. 1503. Windsor Castle, Royal Library
(No. 12685 r. detail: In the upper left corner *Vinci*, in the lower right corner *Florence*).

I. DRAFT OF A LETTER FROM LEONARDO TO LUDOVICO SFORZA, IN WHICH HE OFFERS HIS SERVICES AND STATES HIS ABILITIES; c. 1482.

Most Illustrious Lord, Having now sufficiently considered the specimens of all those who proclaim themselves skilled contrivers of instruments of war, and that the invention and operation of the said instruments are nothing different from those in common use: I shall endeavour, without prejudice to any one else, to explain myself to your Excellency, showing your Lordship my secrets, and then offering them to your best pleasure and approbation to work with effect at opportune moments on all those things which, in part, shall be briefly noted below.

(1) I have a sort of extremely light and strong bridges, adapted to be most easily carried, and with them you may pursue, and at any time flee from the enemy; and others, secure and indestructible by fire and battle, easy and convenient to lift and place. Also methods of burning and destroying those of the enemy.

(2) I know how, when a place is besieged, to take the water out of the trenches, and make endless variety of bridges and covered ways and ladders, and other machines pertaining to such expeditions.

(3) Item. If, by reason of the height of the banks, or the strength of the place, and its position, it is impossible, when besieging a place, to avail oneself of the plan of bombardment, I have methods for destroying every rock or other fortress, even if it were founded on a rock, &c.

(4) Again, I have kinds of mortars, most convenient and easy to carry; and with these I can fling small stones almost resembling a storm; and with the smoke of these cause great terror to the enemy, to his great detriment and confusion.

(5) Item. I have means by secret and tortuous mines and ways, made without noise, to reach a designated [spot], even if it were needed to pass under a trench or a river.

(6) Item. I will make covered chariots, safe and unassailable, which, entering among the enemy with their artillery, there is no body of man so great but they would break them. And behind these, infantry could follow quite unhurt and without any hindrance.

(7) Item. In case of need I will make big guns, mortars, and light ordnance of fine and useful forms, out of the common type.

(8) Where the operation of bombardment might fail, I would contrive catapults, mangonels, *trabocchi*, and other machines of marvellous efficacy and not in common use. And in short, according to the variety of cases, I can contrive various and endless means of offence and defence.

(9) And if the fight should be at sea I have many kinds of machines most efficient for offence and defence; and vessels which will resist the attack of the largest guns and powder and fumes.

(10) In time of peace I believe I can give perfect satisfaction and to the equal of any other in architecture and the composition of buildings public and private; and in guiding water from one place to another.

Item. I can carry out sculpture in marble, bronze, or clay, and also I can do in painting whatever may be done, as well as any other, be he who he may.

Again, the bronze horse may be taken in hand, which is to be to the immortal glory and eternal honour of the prince your father of happy memory, and of the illustrious house of Sforza.

And if any of the above-named things seem to any one to be impossible or not feasible, I am most ready to make the experiment in your park, or in whatever place may please your Excellency – to whom I commend myself with the utmost humility, &c.

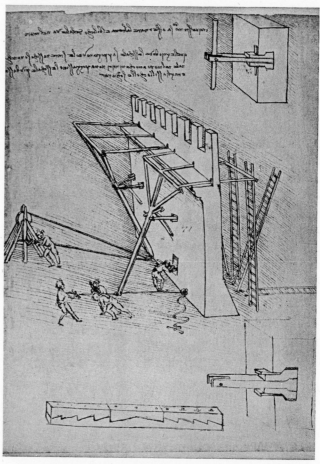

Device against storm ladders. Pen and ink drawing by Leonardo (Codex Atlanticus, 49 v.–b).

II. A Letter from the Florentine Ambassador in Milan to his master, Lorenzo de' Medici, 22 July, 1489; concerning the Sforza Monument.

The Duke Ludovico is planning to erect a worthy monument to his father, and in accordance with his orders Leonardo has been asked to make a model in the form of a large horse (to be cast in bronze), ridden by the Duke Francesco in full armour. As His Highness has in mind something wonderful, the like of which has never been seen, he has directed me to write to you and ask if you will kindly send him one or two Florentine artists who specialize in this kind of work. For, although the Duke has given the commission to Leonardo, it seems to me that he is not confident that he will succeed.

III. From Leonardo's Note-books, concerning the Sforza Monument.

'On the 23rd of April, 1490 . . . I started the horse afresh.'

IV. From the draft of a letter by Leonardo to the Duke Ludovico Sforza, c. 1498.

. . . It vexes me greatly that having to earn my living has forced me to interrupt the work and to attend to small matters, instead of following up the work which your Lordship entrusted to me. But I hope in a short time to have earned so much that I may carry it out quietly to the satisfaction of your Excellency, to whom I commend myself; and if your Lordship thought that I had money, your Lordship was deceived, because I had to feed 6 men for 36 months, and have had only 50 ducats.

V. Ercole I d'Este, Duke of Ferrara, to his agent in Milan, 19 September, 1501; Concerning the model of the Sforza Monument.

Seeing that there exists at Milan a model of a horse, executed by a certain Messer Leonardo, a master very skilful in such matters, one which the Duke Ludovico always intended to have cast, we think that, if the use were granted us of this model, it would be a good and desirable thing to make a casting from it. Therefore, we wish you to go immediately to the most illustrious and reverend the Lord Cardinal of Rouen, and acquaint him with our desire, begging his reverend lordship, if he do not need the said model himself, to be so good as to make it over to us. We would not deprive him of anything that he holds valuable, yet we are persuaded that he cares but little for this work. You may add, likewise, that this will be very agreeable to us for the reasons aforesaid; and that we would gladly be at pains to remove it, bearing in mind that the said model at Milan is, as you have told us, falling daily into decay, there being no care taken of it. If the very reverend lord will gratify us, as we hope, in this matter, we will send persons to bring the said model hither with all care and due precaution, so that it come by no hurt. Do not fail to employ all your good offices that our petition may be granted by his very reverend lordship, to whom we proffer our offers of service and our humble duty.

The Cardinal of Rouen was an uncle of the French governor of Milan. – A model of the equestrian monument was exhibited in 1493, on the occasion of the marriage of the Emperor Maximilian with Bianca Maria Sforza in Milan. When the French entered the town, the Gascon bowmen used this clay model as a target and 'destroyed' it, as Sabba da Castiglione and Vasari have recorded. But, as a year later the Duke of Ferrara asked for the model of the horse, we may assume that it had been only badly damaged.

VI. From the answer of Giovanni Valla, the agent of Ercole I d'Este, Milan, 24 December, 1501.

With reference to the model of the horse erected by Duke Ludovico, as far as he is concerned, his reverend lordship perfectly agrees to its removal; yet as his Majesty the King had himself seen the statue, his lordship dare not grant the Duke's request without previously informing the King.

VII. The Duke, Ludovico Sforza, to his secretary Domino Marchesino Stanga; concerning the 'Last Supper'.

We have entrusted to you the carrying out of the matters mentioned on the enclosed list; and, although our orders were delivered to you by word of mouth, it shall add to our comfort that we set them down in these few words to inform you how extraordinary is our interest in their execution.

LUDOVICO MARIA SFORTIA

Milan, the 29th of June, 1497.

The 'memoriale' appended to this letter mentions thirteen different matters, the greater portion referring to works of art. One of the points is:

'Item. Of Leonardo of Florence it is to be solicited that he finish the work in the Refettorio delle Gratie, when he must set to work upon the other front wall* thereof, which if he can do, the agreements previously signed by him respecting its completion within a given time will be cancelled.' (*See Appendix plate II.)

VIII. Concerning the 'Last Supper'. From a tale by Matteo Bandello ('Novelle', Lucca 1554).

In Ludovico's time, some gentlemen living in Milan

Madonna with the laughing Child. Terracotta. About 1470–75. (Attributed to Leonardo by Carotti, Sirén, Valentiner, Middeldorf, Venturi, Heydenreich, and John Goldsmith Phillips.) London, Victoria and Albert Museum.

The Madonna with the Yarn-winder. Composed in 1501. (Attributed to Leonardo by Emil Möller, 1926, and by Cecil Gould, 1957.)
Drumlanrig Castle, Scotland, The Duke of Buccleuch.

were met one day in the monks' refectory of the convent delle Grazie, where with hushed voices they watched Leonardo da Vinci as he was finishing his marvellous picture of the *Last Supper*. The painter was well pleased that each should tell him what they thought of his work. He would often come to the convent at early dawn; and this I have seen him do myself. Hastily mounting the scaffolding, he worked diligently until the shades of evening compelled him to cease, never thinking to take food at all, so absorbed was he in his work. At other times he would remain there three or four days without touching his picture, only coming for a few hours to remain before it, with folded arms, gazing at his figures as if to criticize them himself. At mid-day, too, when the glare of a sun at its zenith has made barren all the streets of Milan, I have seen him hasten from the citadel, where he was modelling his colossal horse, without seeking the shade, by the shortest way to the convent, where he would add a touch or two and immediately return.

Matteo Bandello was a nephew of Vincenzo, the prior of the Dominican monastery of Santa Maria della Grazie. In 1495, when he was about fifteen, he came to Milan and was placed in the care of his uncle; two years later he became acquainted with Leonardo, who was then painting the 'Last Supper' in the refectory of the Church belonging to the monks whose prior was Bandello's uncle.

IX. LEONARDO IN VENICE. A LETTER FROM LORENZO GUSNASCO, MAKER OF MUSICAL INSTRUMENTS, TO ISABELLA D'ESTE.

Most illustrious Lady, I am sending you by this courier an excellent lute of walnut wood, made in the Spanish fashion, which seems to me to have the finest tone I ever heard. I have been ill and unable to finish the other lute . . .

Leonardo da Vinci, who is in Venice, has shewed to me a portrait of your Highness, which is in every way a most truthful likeness. Indeed it is so well executed that nothing could be better. This is all that I write by this post, and with the repeated assurance of my respect,
I beg to subscribe myself,
Your Highness's faithful servant,

Venice, 13th March, 1500   LORENZO DA PAVIA

Leonardo's portrait of Isabella d'Este is mentioned by Père Dan (Trésor des merveilles de Fontainebleau, 1642) as being in the collection of Francis the First, King of France.– Cf. plate 24.

X. FROM A LETTER OF ISABELLA D'ESTE, 27 MARCH, 1501, TO FRA PIETRO DA NOVELLARA; CONCERNING A MADONNA PAINTING AND A PORTRAIT.

Ascertain whether he is inclined to paint a picture for

our studio. If he consents, we will leave the invention and the time to his decision. If he is reluctant, try at least to induce him to paint for us a small picture of the Madonna, pious and sweet, as is his style. And then ask him to send us a new sketch of our portrait. For his Highness, our consort, has given away the one he left for us here.

The studio of the duchess was on the ground floor of the Palazzo di Corte at Mantua. For this studio Mantegna, Correggio, Perugino and Costa painted nine pictures. Leonardo did nothing. In 1504, however, he accepted the commission to paint an Infant Christ for Isabella (see note on plate 7, p. 152).

XI. A LETTER FROM FRA PIETRO DA NOVELLARA TO MARCHESA ISABELLA D'ESTE OF MANTUA, APRIL 8TH, 1501; CONCERNING 'THE CARTOON OF ST ANNE'.

Leonardo's life is changeful and uncertain; it is thought that he lives only for the day. Since he has been in Florence, he has worked just on one cartoon, which represents an infant Christ of about one year, freeing himself almost out of his mother's arms and seizing a lamb and apparently about to embrace it. The mother half rising from the lap of St Anne is catching the child to draw it away from the lamb, that sacrificial animal which signifies the Passion. St Anne, just rising from her seat, as if she would wish to hinder her daughter from parting the Child from the lamb; which perhaps signifies the Church that would not wish the Passion of Christ to be hindered. The figures are life-size, but they fill only a small cartoon, because all are seated or bent, and each one is placed before the other, to the left. The sketch is not yet complete. He has done nothing else, except that he now and then lends a hand to one or another of the portraits which his two assistants are painting. He is entirely wrapped up in geometry and has no patience for painting.

Novellara describes a lost cartoon of St Anne. See the note on plate 54. Concerning his important remark on Leonardo's touching up portraits by his pupils, compare plate 27.

XII. A LETTER FROM FRA PIETRO DA NOVELLARA, TO MARCHESA ISABELLA D'ESTE OF MANTUA, 14 APRIL, 1501; CONCERNING 'THE MADONNA WITH THE YARN-WINDER'.

I have this week heard, through his pupil Salai and other of his friends, of Leonardo the artist's decision, which led me to visit him on the Wednesday of Passion Week in order to assure myself that it was true. In brief, his mathematical experiments have made painting so distasteful to him that he cannot even bear to take up a brush. However, I tried all I could, using first every art in order to get him to accede to your highness's wishes; and when I saw that he seemed well-disposed to place himself under obligation to your Eminence, I frankly told him everything, and we came to the following understanding, viz.: that, if he should be able to release himself from his engagement with the King of France without thereby forfeiting that monarch's goodwill (which he hoped might be managed in, at the most, a month's time), he would serve your Eminence in preference to any one else in the world. In any case, however, he will at once paint the portrait and forward it to your Eminence, as the small picture which he had to execute for one Robertet, a favourite of the King of France, is now finished. I left two with him, in order to expedite matters. The little picture represents a Madonna seated, and at work with a spindle, while the Infant Christ, with one foot upon the basket of flax, holds it by the handle, and looks with wonder at four rays of light, which fall in the form of a cross, as if wishing for them. Smilingly, he grasps the spindle, which he seeks to withhold from his mother. Thus much I was able to fix with him. I preached my sermon yesterday. God grant that it may bring forth rich fruit, for the hearers were numerous. I commend myself to your Eminence.

FRATER PETRUS DE NUVOLARIA
Vice-General of the Carmelite Monks.
Florence, April 14th, 1501.

See Burlington Magazine, vol. XLIX, August 1926, pp. 61–68, Emil Möller, 'The Madonna with the Yarn-winder', in the possession of the Duke of Buccleuch (see the illustration on p. 36). Another copy is in the collection of Robert W. Reford in Montreal, Canada. As of the 'St Anne', Leonardo designed two versions of the 'Madonna with the Yarn-winder', one with the Christ Child on the left, and one with the Child on the right. Copies of both versions are extant.

XIII LETTERS PATENT ISSUED TO LEONARDO BY CESARE BORGIA. PAVIA, 8TH AUGUST, 1502.

To all those of our *locotenenti, castellani, officiali* and *subditi*, whom it may concern, we herewith charge and command them, that they everywhere and in every place give free entrance to our highly-esteemed court architect Leonardo da Vinci, the bearer of this, who has been commissioned by us to inspect the fortresses and strongholds of our states, and to make such alterations and improvements as he may think needful. Both he and his followers are to be received with hospitality, and every facility afforded him for personal inspection, for measurement and valuation, just as he may wish. For that purpose a band of men is to be placed at his disposal, which is to give him all the help that he may require. With reference to the state works already in course of completion, we desire that every engineer be

prepared to further any undertaking which he may find necessary.

XIV. A LETTER FROM FRANCESCO PANDOLFINI, FLORENTINE AMBASSADOR AT THE FRENCH COURT, FROM BLOIS, 22 JANUARY, 1507.

Finding myself this morning in the presence of the most Christian King, his Majesty called me and said: 'Your lords must render me a service. Write to them that I desire to make use of their painter, Master Leonardo, who is now at Milan, and that I wish him to do certain things for me. Do this in such a way that their lordships enjoin him to serve me promptly and tell him not to depart from Milan before my arrival. He is a good master, and I desire certain things by his hand. Write to Florence at once, and in such a way as to obtain the desired result, and send me the letter.' All this came from a little painting by his hand that has recently been brought here, and which is judged to be a very excellent work. In the course of conversation I asked his Majesty what works he desired from him, and he answered, 'Certain small pictures of Our Lady and others, according as the idea occurs to me: perhaps I shall get him to paint my portrait.'

XV. DRAFT OF A LETTER FROM LEONARDO TO THE DUKE OF NEMOURS, GIULIANO DE' MEDICI, THE BROTHER OF LEO X.

I was so greatly rejoiced, most Illustrious Lord, by the desired restoration of your health that it almost had the effect that my own health recovered. . . . But I am extremely vexed that I have not been able completely to satisfy the wishes of your Excellency, by reason of the wickedness of that deceiver, for whom I left nothing undone which could be done for him by me and by which I might be of use to him; and in the first place his allowances were paid to him before the time, which I believe he would willingly deny, if I had not the writing signed by myself and the interpreter. And I, seeing that he did not work for me unless he had no work to do for others, which he was very careful in soliciting, invited him to eat with me, and to work afterwards near me, because, besides saving of expense, he would acquire the Italian language. (He always promised, but would never do so.) And this I did also, because that young German who makes the mirrors, was there always in the workshop, and wanted to see and to know all that was being done there and made it known outside blaming what he did not understand and because he dined with those of the Pope's guard, and then they went out with guns killing birds among the ruins; and this went on from after dinner till the evening; and when I sent Lorenzo to urge him to work he said that he would not have so many masters over him, and that his work was for Your Excellency's Wardrobe; and thus two months passed and so it went on; and one day finding Gian Niccolo of the Wardrobe and asking whether the German had finished the work for your Magnificence, he told me this was not true, but only that he had given him two guns to clean. Afterwards, when I urged him further, he left the workshop and began to work in his room, and lost much time in making another pair of pincers and files and other tools with screws; and there he worked at reels for twisting silk which he hid when any one of my people went in, and with a thousand oaths and mutterings, so that none of them would go there any more.

Written in Rome, c. 1514, while Leonardo was living in the Belvedere of the Vatican. There is another draft for the same letter extant, showing the same nervous irritation.

XVI. THE VISIT OF THE CARDINAL LUIGI D'ARAGONA, PAID TO LEONARDO, ON 10 OCTOBER, 1517; TOLD BY HIS SECRETARY, ANTONIO DE' BEATIS.

On the 10th of October, 1517, Monsignor and the rest of us went to see, in one of the outlying parts of the Amboise, Messer Leonardo Vinci the Florentine, a grey-beard of more than seventy years, the most eminent painter of our time, who showed to his Eminence the Cardinal three pictures: one of a certain Florentine lady, painted from life, at the instance of the late Lord Giuliano de' Medici; the other of the youthful St John the Baptist; and the third of the Madonna and the Child in the lap of St Anne, the most perfect of them all. One cannot indeed expect any more good work from him, as a certain paralysis has crippled his right hand. But he has a pupil, a Milanese, who works well enough: and although Messer Leonardo can no longer paint with the sweetness which was peculiar to him, he can still design and instruct others. This gentleman has written a treatise on anatomy, showing by illustrations the members, muscles, nerves, veins, joints, intestines, and whatever else is to discuss in the bodies of men and women, in a way that has never yet been done by any one else. All this we have seen with our own eyes; and he said that he had dissected more than thirty bodies, both of men and women of all ages. He has also written of the nature of water, and of divers machines, and of other matters, which he has set down in an endless number of volumes, all in the vulgar tongue, which, if they be published, will be profitable and delightful.

St Anne, see plate 68; St John, see plate 55. The portrait of 'a certain Florentine lady' was most probably the Mona Lisa (plate 28). The 'Milanese pupil' is Francesco Melzi.

XVII. LETTER FROM FRANCESCO MELZI TO THE BROTHERS OF LEONARDO, ABOUT THE DEATH OF THE MASTER.

To Ser Giuliano and his honoured brothers –

I believe that the death of your brother, Maestro Leonardo, has already been certified to you. He was to me the best of fathers, and it is impossible for me to express the grief that his death has caused me. Until the day when my body is laid under the ground, I shall experience perpetual sorrow, and not without reason, for he daily showed me the most devoted and warmest affection.

His loss is a grief to everyone, for it is not in the power of nature to reproduce another such man. May the Almighty accord him everlasting rest. He passed from the present life on the 2nd of May with all the sacraments of holy Mother Church, and well disposed to receive them. The reason that he was able to make a will, leaving his goods to whom he liked, was on account of his possessing a letter from the king, exempting him *quod heredes supplicantis sint regnicolae*. Without such a letter he would not have been able to will away anything he possessed here, this being the custom of the country. Maestro Leonardo accordingly made his will, which I should have sent you sooner had I been able to confide it to a trustworthy person. I expect that one of my uncles who has been to see me will soon return to Milan. I will dispose it in his hands, and he will faithfully remit it to you. Up to the present time I have not found other means of sending it. In so much as concerns your part in the will, Maestro Leonardo possessed in the [hospital of] Santa Maria Nuova, in the hands of the treasurer, four hundred gold crowns (*scudi di sole*) in notes which have been placed out at five per cent for the last six years counting from last October. He had also an estate at Fiesole that he wished to be distributed equally among you. There is nothing more concerning you in the will, and I will say no more except to offer you my most willing service. You will find me ready and anxious to do your will.

I recommend myself continually to you.

Given at Amboise, the 1st of June, 1519.
   Please reply by the Gondi,
                            Tanquam fratri vestro,
                            Franciscus Meltius

CHRONOLOGY OF LEONARDO'S LIFE

I. FIRST FLORENTINE PERIOD: 1452–1481

1452 (15 April) Leonardo born in Anchiano, outside Vinci, near Florence; the illegitimate son of Ser Piero da Vinci and Caterina, a peasant girl. Leonardo's father marries in the same year a young woman of a rich family.

1457 Leonardo's mother marries a peasant. The child is taken into Ser Piero's household, where he lives with his grandparents, and a married uncle, and is nursed by a childless stepmother. (Leonardo's father married four times and had eleven children by his third and fourth wives.)

Leonardo is mentioned in the 1457 taxation return of his grandfather as an illegitimate son of Ser Piero.

1469 Leonardo is mentioned again in the taxation return of the Vinci family.

Ser Piero becomes notary to the Signoria and moves with his family to Florence; Leonardo enters Verrocchio's workshop.

1472 Leonardo's name entered in the Red Book of Painters of Florence, as a member of the Guild of St Luke. He is now entitled to accept commissions of his own but stays as an assistant in Verrocchio's workshop.

The *'Annunciation'* (plate 59).

1473 Dated Landscape drawing (plate 81). The *'Kneeling Angel'* (plate 43).

1476 Leonardo accused of sodomy with a model, Jacopo Santarelli. This accusation is dismissed (7 June, 1476) with the condition that it might be brought up again on further evidence. He is mentioned twice in this year as living in Verrocchio's house. Verrocchio competes for the commission of the Forteguerri monument; his model is accepted. (Valentiner claimed that Leonardo collaborated in this sculpture.)

1478 (10 January) Leonardo receives a commission for the altarpiece of the St Bernard chapel in the Palazzo Vecchio.

(14 March) First payment for this painting (which he soon abandons).

(Autumn) Drawing with note by Leonardo: '... *bre* 1478 *inchominciai le 2 S. Vergine Marie* ...' (which means that Leonardo began two Madonna paintings or reliefs in autumn 1478). Underneath is a line of which half is torn off; we can just read, '... *e chompa in Pistoia*' (the meaning is probably that the one Madonna was begun in Florence, the other in Pistoia).

The *'Madonna di Piazza'* for the Duomo in Pistoia is painted in Verrocchio's workshop (illustrated, p. 27). Verrocchio works (with the help of Leonardo?) on the *'Careggi Resurrection'* relief (plate VII).

1479 Leonardo's drawing of Baroncelli hanging by his neck from a window of the Bargello. (The commission to paint in fresco the hanging of the murderers of Giuliano de' Medici is given to Botticelli.)

Leonardo *'in casa propria'*, his own lodgings; he does not stay any longer with Verrocchio or Ser Piero.

1481 (March) Leonardo is commissioned by the monks of San Donato a Scopeto to paint *The Adoration of the Kings* for the high-altar of their monastery (plate 49). He also decorates their clock; the monks buy him some ultramarine for this job.

(28 September) Last payment for the *Adoration of the Kings*; the picture remains unfinished.

Leonardo offers in a letter his services (as engineer, architect and sculptor) to Ludovico Sforza, the ruler of Milan (Document I, p. 33).

Verrocchio sends his model for the horse of *Colleoni* to Venice.

II. FIRST MILANESE PERIOD: 1482–1499

1482 Leonardo moves to Milan. (The Anonimo Gaddiano says: 'When he was thirty'.) He brings a lute, a present from Lorenzo de' Medici, and is accompanied by the musician Migliorotti.

1483 (25 April) Contract for the *'Virgin of the Rocks'*, given by the Confraternity of the Immaculate Conception in S. Francesco Grande at Milan to three painters – Leonardo, and the brothers Evangelista and Ambrogio de' Predis (plate 64 and plate 65).

Leonardo paints the portrait of Cecilia Gallerani, the mistress of Ludovico Sforza (plate 22).

Leonardo begins his work on the equestrian monument for Francesco Sforza (on which, according to Sabba da Castiglione, he worked for sixteen years).

1485 (26 March) Leonardo studies the total eclipse of the sun.

(13 April) Ludovico Sforza commissions Leonardo to paint an *'Adoration of the Child'* for Matthias Corvinus, King of Hungary.

1487 Payments to Leonardo for a wooden model for the tambour of the dome of the Cathedral in Milan.

1488 Death of Verrocchio in Venice, before the casting of his *Colleoni* is carried out.

1489 Anatomical studies (MS. B.).

1490 (13 January) Leonardo designs dresses for the Court on the occasion of the marriage of Gian Galeazzo Sforza, and other decorations, including even horse-trappings. *'Il Paradiso'* by the court poet Bernardo Bellinzone, is performed; the stage design is by Leonardo.

A note by Leonardo's hand (in MS. C, folio 15): *'A di 23 aprile 1490 cominciai questo libro e ricominciai il cavallo'* '(I have started this book and re-started to work on the equestrian monument').

(8 June) In Pavia with Francesco di Giorgio, consulted in connection with the Duomo. He admires the 'Regisole', the equestrian monument at Pavia (Richter §1445).

(22 July) Salai, a boy of ten, joins Leonardo as his servant and pupil; he remains with him for twenty-five years.

1491 (26 January, and the following days) 'Tournament', staged by Galeazzo Sanseverino in honour of the wedding of Ludovico Sforza and Beatrice d'Este; designed by Leonardo.

(2 April) Boltraffio mentioned as in Leonardo's studio.

1492 A short visit to Rome.

Death of Lorenzo de' Medici.

1493 (30 November) Leonardo's huge clay model for the horse of the Sforza monument is exhibited during the marriage festivities for Bianca Maria Sforza and Emperor Maximilian.

1494 A French army invades Italy. The Medici expelled from Florence. (They return in 1512.)

Luca Pacioli publishes his 'Summa arithmetica'.

1495 Leonardo working on The Last Supper (plate 73).

He teaches himself Latin.

(Summer) Short visit to Florence.

1496 (31 January) In the Palazzo of Gian Francesco Sanseverino at Milan, in the presence of the Duke, a play on Danae, by Baldassare Taccone, is performed. Leonardo designed the scenery. Luca Pacioli, professor of mathematics, moves to Milan and becomes friends with Leonardo.

Baldassare Castiglione, the 'complete gentleman', moves from the Court of Mantua to the Court of Milan.

1497 (29 June) Leonardo still working on The Last Supper. He paints in oil, on the opposite wall, the portraits of Ludovico Sforza and his family (in the corners of Montorfano's Crucifixion fresco; plate II).

1498 Savonarola hanged, and then burned on the stake.

Leonardo's murals in the Sala delle Asse.

(2 October) Ludovico Sforza gives Leonardo a vineyard.

(December) Short visit to Mantua.

1499 (6 October) Occupation of Milan by a French army under Trivulzio; the Duke has fled from his town a few days earlier.

(14 December) Leonardo sends 600 gold florins for his account to Florence, and soon after that he returns there by way of Mantua and Venice. Luca Pacioli is in his company.

III. SECOND FLORENTINE PERIOD: 1500–1506

1500 (February) In Mantua; draws the portrait of Isabella d'Este (plate 24).

(March) In Venice. Lorenzo Gusnasco, a maker of musical instruments, writes to Isabella d'Este that he has seen her portrait, painted by Leonardo ('molto naturale, tanto bene fatto, non è possibile meglio'. See Document IX, p. 37).

(10 April) Ludovico Sforza, who had returned to Milan with an army of Swiss and German mercenaries, is defeated and taken prisoner.

(24 April) Leonardo, back in Florence, draws there 50 gold florins from his account at the Ospedale di S. Maria Nuova.

(Leonardo had left Florence when he was thirty, now he is forty-eight. There is a scarcity of good artists in Florence; Verrocchio, Luca della Robbia, Bertoldo, the brothers Pollaiuolo, Domenico Ghirlandaio, and Botticini are dead now; young Michelangelo is in Rome, where he has just finished his Pietà of St Peter's; the best artists in Florence are Andrea della Robbia, Piero di Cosimo, Fra Bartolommeo, Botticelli, Lorenzo di Credi, and Filippino Lippi. Leonardo has to his credit hardly more than the Last Supper and the model of the large Horse. He will stay in Florence only seven years.)

1501 (April) Letters from Fra Pietro da Novellara to Isabella d'Este concerning Leonardo's cartoon of St Anne, a Madonna with the Yarnwinder, and about portraits painted by pupils and touched up by Leonardo (Documents XI and XII; and the illustration on p. 36).

1502 (probably from July onward, about eight months) Leonardo as military engineer in the service of Cesare Borgia on his campaign in Central Italy.

1503 (4 March) Leonardo has returned to Florence and draws some money from his account at the Ospedale di S. Maria Nuova. His luggage is still at the custom-house (Richter §§ 1420, 1444, 1454); he is in connection with several artists – Lorenzo di Credi, Filippino Lippi, Piero di Cosimo, and others –, and he also mentions in these notes Lorenzo di Pierfrancesco de' Medici (who died later in this year, 20 May). Leonardo, now over fifty, needs spectacles (mentioned three times in these notes). In the same notes Leonardo mentions "my map of the world which Giovanni Benci has", and the name "Piero dal Borgo", which could mean Piero della Francesca's manuscript on perspective (see under 1509).

(8 October) Rejoins the Guild of Painters in Florence. A mural The Battle of Anghiari commissioned by the Signoria of Florence (plates 108–110).

The portrait of Mona Lisa (plate 28).

1504 (25 January) Leonardo – together with Botticelli, Cosimo Rosselli, Piero di Cosimo, and other artists – in a committee appointed to decide the best position for Michelangelo's David. (With this sculpture and the cartoon of the Battle of Cascina to his credit, Michelangelo, 23 years younger than Leonardo, begins to obscure Leonardo's fame in Florence.)

(9 July) Death of Leonardo's father.

Young Raphael in Florence.

1505 (30 April) The Signoria pays 11 Lire for ochre, gypsum and sponges: Leonardo has finished the cartoon for The Battle of Anghiari and begins the painting of the mural.

The Signoria pays at the custom house in Florence the expenses for the transport of some garments which have come from Rome and belong to Leonardo.

Leonardo studies the flights of birds and stereometry.

(31 August and 31 October) Last payments for materials for the Anghiari mural.

1506 (20 May) Leonardo has spent 450 gold florins, out of the savings of 600 he had made in Milan.

Leonardo invited to Milan by the French Governor Charles d'Amboise, Count de Chaumont.

IV. SECOND MILANESE PERIOD: 1506–1513

1506 (June) Leonardo in Milan. He paints a small picture of the Madonna which enchants the King.

He is appointed painter and engineer to Louis XII.

He begins, assisted by pupils, the second version of *The Madonna of the Rocks* (plate 65).

1507 (20 April) The vineyard, once given by Ludovico Sforza to Leonardo, is restituted to him.

(September) Leonardo returns to Florence; stays for about six months in the Casa Martelli and aids the sculptor Rustici in his work (plate V).

1508 (Spring) Back in Milan.

Studies for the Trivulzio monument (plate III; the last sketches for this monument date from 1511).

1509 Luca Pacioli's *De Divina Proportione*, issued in Venice, with 60 illustrations, probably after designs by Leonardo.

1510 Leonardo occupies himself mainly with anatomy and other scientific studies.

1511 Leonardo meets the anatomist Marc Antonio della Torre, who helps him with his researches.

Milan at war with the Pope and Venice.

(Spring) Leonardo back in Florence; writes to Melzi. Letter to Charles d'Amboise, telling him that he will return to Milan at Easter and bring two Madonna paintings for the King.

(Late summer, or autumn) Returns to Milan.

(18 December) Windsor drawing No. 12416: Two studies of a fire in Milan.

1512 The restoration of the Medici in Florence. The French lose Milan; Massimiliano Sforza, son of Ludovico, supported by a coalition of the Pope, Venice and Spain, returns to Milan.

1513 (24 September) Leonardo moves to Rome, accompanied by Melzi, Salai, and two other pupils.

(October) He passes through Florence and deposits some money for his account at the Ospedale di S. Maria Nuova.

V. THE LAST SEVEN YEARS · ROME AND CLOUX:
1513–16; 1517–19

1513 (1 December) Leonardo in the service of Giuliano de' Medici, Duke of Nemours, brother of Pope Leo X.

He lives in the Belvedere of the Vatican.

Raphael on the peak of his fame, working on his *Stanze di Vaticano*. Michelangelo, who has already finished his *Sistine Frescoes*, works on the large marble statue of *Moses*.

1514 Leonardo draws, in black chalk and ink, the visions of the '*Deluge*' (a set of ten drawings at Windsor Castle, Nos. 12377–86; see Plate 85).

1515 (9 January) Death of Leonardo's patron, Giuliano de' Medici, Duke of Nemours.

(October) Francis I, successor of Louis XII, recaptures Milan.

(14 December) Leonardo probably present at a meeting of the Pope and the King of France in Bologna.

1516 (August) Leonardo's note on measurements in the church of S. Paolo, Rome.

(Autumn 1516, or perhaps Spring 1517) Leonardo accepts the invitation of Francis I and departs for France.

1517 Ascension Day in Amboise; May in Cloux.

Lives in the Manoir de Cloux, between the town and the Royal Castle.

(10 October) The Cardinal Luigi d'Aragona visits Leonardo and is shown illustrated manuscripts from Leonardo's hand, and three paintings – a portrait of a Florentine Lady, commissioned by Giuliano de' Medici, Duke of Nemours, a youthful John the Baptist, and a Madonna and Child in the lap of St Anne (Document XVI).

1517–18 Salary payments for two years to Leonardo, Melzi, and Salai.

1518 (19 June) Court festivals at Cloux, repeating Bellinzone's pageant '*Il Paradiso*' of 1490, for which Leonardo made the designs.

1519 (23 April) Leonardo makes his Will (Richter § 1566). The Testator desires to be buried in the church of Saint Florentin at Amboise; he stipulates how many priests and monks should follow the body; he asks that three high and thirty low masses should be celebrated at Saint Florentin for the peace of his soul, and similar services in other churches at Amboise. To Melzi he leaves 'for services and favours done to him in the past' all his instruments and artist's tools, his manuscripts and paintings, also his clothes and money; everything else he bequeathes to Salai and other servants. He names the exact number of candles to be carried at the funeral and says how much wax should be donated to the churches; and he does not forget alms to the poor. To his half-brothers in Florence (with whom, twelve years before, he had fought in court over the division of an inheritance) he bequeathes all the money 'in the hands of the treasurer of Santa Maria Nuova in Florence'.

1519 (2 May) Death of Leonardo. (The King was on this day with the Court at Saint Germain-en-Laye, where he signed a decree on the 1st of May.)

(12 August) Ceremony of Leonardo's burial at the cloister of the church of Saint Florentin at Amboise.

THE PLATES

AN ASTERISK (*) IN FRONT OF THE NUMBER INDICATES THAT THE
REPRODUCTION IS IN THE SAME SIZE AS THE ORIGINAL

1. *Leonardo's Self-Portrait*. Red chalk. About 1512. Turin, Library

*2. *Five Grotesque Heads*. Pen and ink. About 1490. Windsor Castle, Royal Library

*3. *Antique Warrior.* Silverpoint on cream-coloured paper. About 1478. London, British Museum

4. *Heads of Girls, Young and Old Men*. Pen and ink. About 1478–80. Windsor Castle, Royal Library

*5. *Female Half-Figure*, seventeen studies. Silverpoint on red prepared paper. About 1478–80. Windsor Castle, Royal Library

*6. *Old Man thinking*. Pen and ink (slightly enlarged). About 1510. Windsor Castle, Royal Library

*7. *Head of a Pharisee*. Pen and ink, and wash. About 1504. Windsor Castle, Royal Library

*8. *Head of Christ*. Silverpoint. About 1500. Venice, Academy

9. *Head of Christ*. About 1495. Milan, Brera

*10. *Studies for the Leda*. Pen and ink. About 1506. Windsor Castle, Royal Library

*11. *Study for the Leda*. Pen and ink. About 1506. Windsor Castle, Royal Library

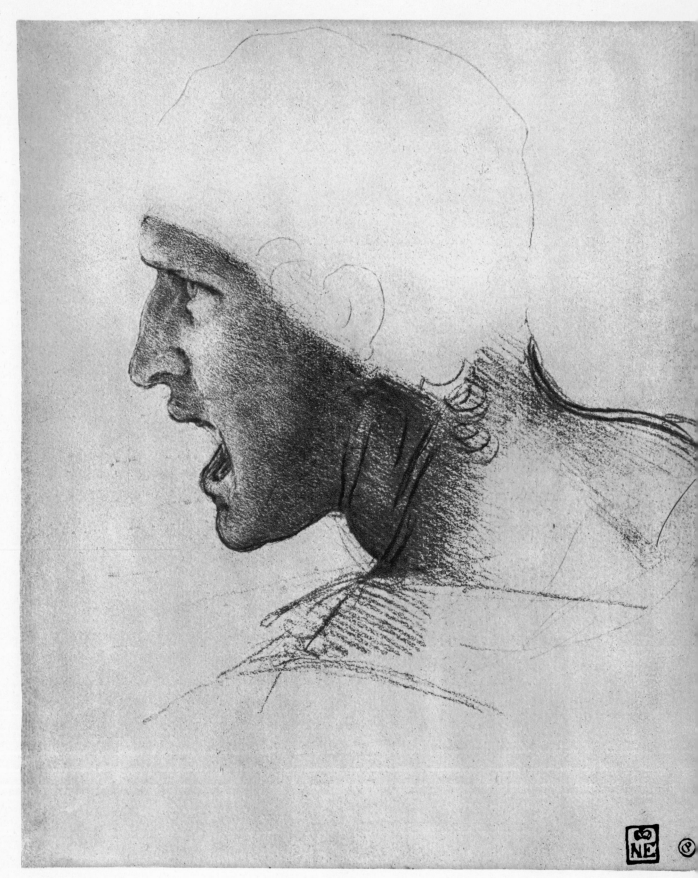

*12. *Head of a Warrior* (Study for the *Battle of Anghiari*). Red chalk. 1503. Budapest, Museum of Fine Arts

*13. *Heads of Warriors* (Study for the *Battle of Anghiari*). Black chalk. 1503. Budapest, Museum of Fine Arts

*14. *Apostle* (Study for the *Last Supper*). Pen and ink, and wash, on blue prepared paper. About 1495. Vienna, Albertina

*15. *St. James the Greater* (Study for the *Last Supper*). Red chalk. 1495–96.
Lower left corner: *The Sforza Castel at Milan*. Pen and ink.
Windsor Castle, Royal Library

*16. *St. Bartholomew* (Study for the *Last Supper*). Red chalk on red paper. 1495–96.
Windsor Castle, Royal Library

*17. *St. Philip* (Study for the *Last Supper*). Black chalk. 1495–96.
Windsor Castle, Royal Library

*18. *St. Anne*. Red chalk on brownish paper, heightened with white. About 1501. Windsor Castle, Royal Library

*19. *Head of a Young Woman.* Silverpoint on blue prepared paper (partly worked over by a pupil). About 1486.
Windsor Castle, Royal Library

*20. *Study for the Angel's Head in the Virgin of the Rocks*, Louvre (cf. Plate 21). Silverpoint on light brown prepared paper, heightened with white. 1483. Turin, Royal Library

*21. *Angel's Head*. Detail from Plate 64.

22. *Portrait of a Lady with an Ermine*. About 1483. Cracow, Museum Czartoryski

23. *Portrait of Ginevra de' Benci*. About 1474–78. Vaduz, Liechtenstein Gallery

24. *Supposed Portrait of Isabella d'Este*. Black chalk and pastel, touches of yellow in dress, red in hair, heightened with white. (Detail.) About 1500. Paris, Louvre

25. *Portrait of a Girl with a Cap.* Silverpoint on pinkish paper. About 1493–95. Windsor Castle, Royal Library

26. *Portrait of a Musician*. Unfinished. About 1485. Milan, Ambrosiana

27. Ambrogio de Predis and Leonardo: *Portrait of a Lady*. About 1490. Milan, Ambrosiana

28. *Mona Lisa.* 1503. Paris, Louvre

30. *Mona Lisa*. Detail from Plate 28

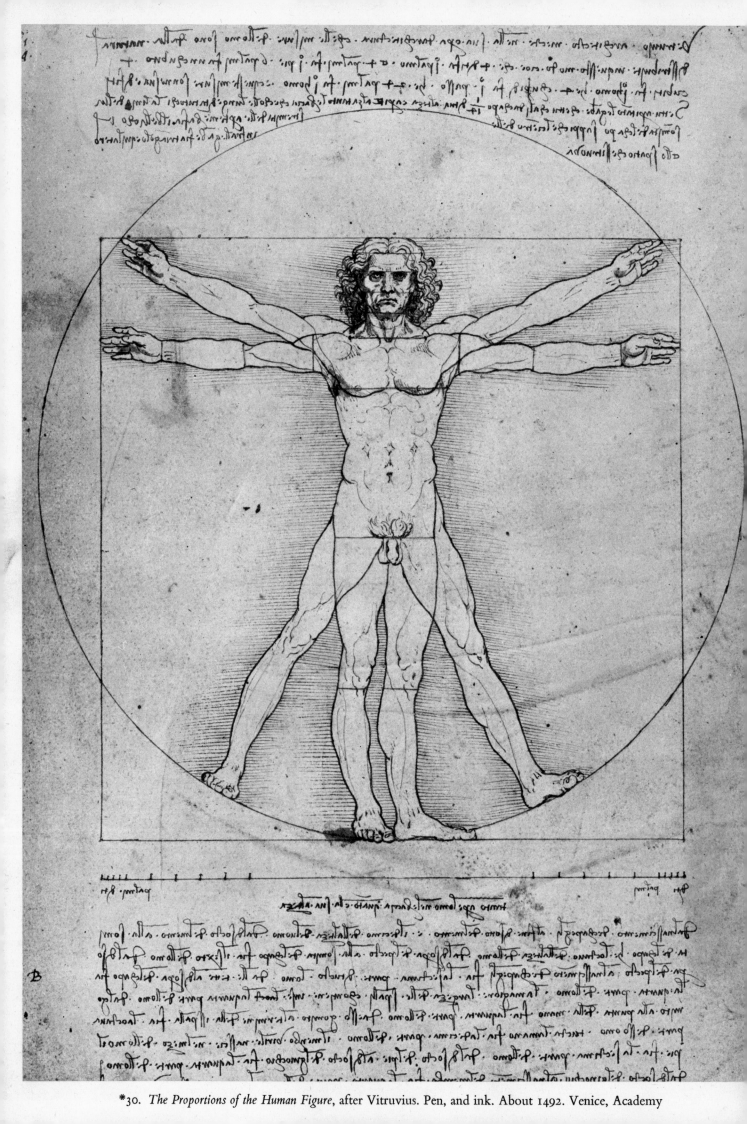

*30. *The Proportions of the Human Figure*, after Vitruvius. Pen, and ink. About 1492. Venice, Academy

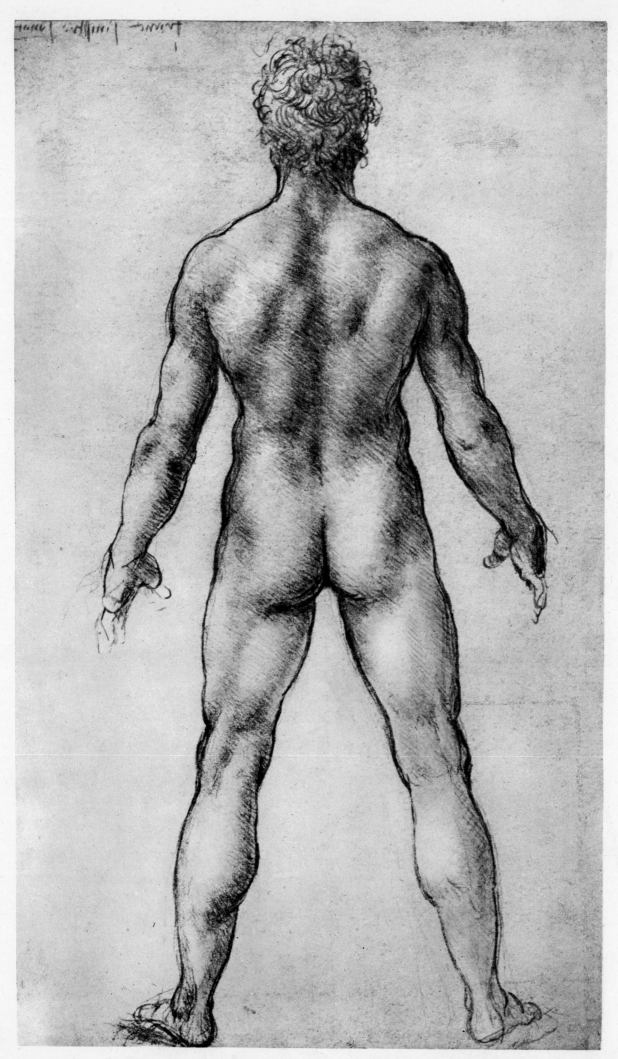

*31. *Nude Figure of a Man*. Red chalk. About 1503. Windsor Castle, Royal Library

*32. *Studies of Hands*. Silverpoint on pink prepared paper. About 1481. Windsor Castle, Royal Library

*33. *Study of a Woman's Hands folded over her Breast*. Silverpoint on pink prepared paper, heightened with white.
About 1478. Windsor Castle, Royal Library

*34. *Pointing Woman in Landscape*. Brownish chalk. About 1513. Windsor Castle, Royal Library

*35. *Youth in a Masquerade Costume*. Pen and ink, wash, over black chalk. About 1506–7. Windsor Castle, Royal Library

***36. *Leda and the Swan*. Pen and bistre, and wash, over black chalk, about 1504–06.
Chatsworth, Devonshire Collection**

37. *Leda and the Swan*. Free copy of a lost painting by Leonardo of about 1506. Rome, Spiridon Collection

*38. *Drapery Study for a kneeling Woman*. Brush drawing in black and white on blue paper. About 1483–86.
Windsor Castle, Royal Library

*39. *Drapery Study for a kneeling Woman.* Silverpoint, heightened with white, on red prepared paper. About 1477.
Rome, Corsini Gallery

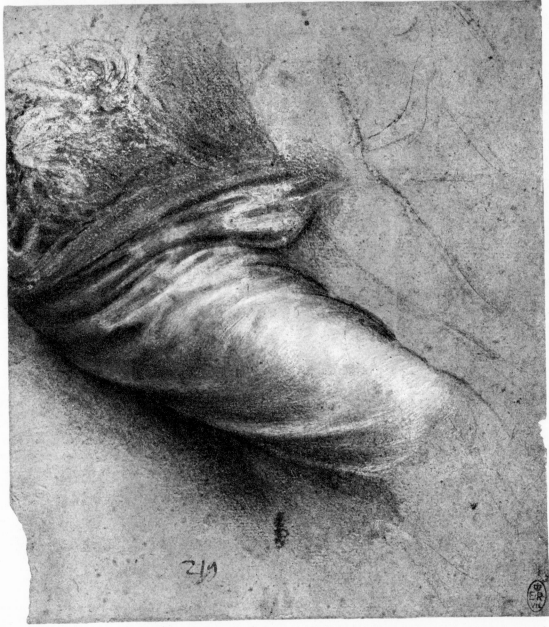

*40 and *41. *Drapery Studies* (for the Madonna in the *St. Anne* painting, Plate 68). About 1508.
Windsor Castle, Royal Library

*42. *Study of Drapery* (for the right arm of St. Peter, Plate 73). Black chalk, heightened with white. About 1496.
Windsor Castle, Royal Library

43. *Kneeling Angel in Profile.* About 1473. (Contributed by Leonardo to Verrocchio's *Baptism of Christ.*) Florence, Uffizi

*44. *St. John the Baptist*. Silverpoint, heightened with white, on blue prepared paper.
About 1478. Windsor Castle, Royal Library

*45. *Three Dancing Maidens*. Pen and ink. About 1503. Venice, Academy

46. *Neptune*. Black chalk. About 1504. Windsor Castle, Royal Library

*47. *Allegory of Fortune*. Silverpoint, pen and ink, and wash. About 1483. London, British Museum

*48. *Study for the Adoration of the Kings* (Plate 49). Pen and ink. About 1481. Paris, Louvre

49. *The Adoration of the Kings*. (Unfinished.) About 1481–82. Florence, Uffizi

52. Detail from Plate 49

53. Detail from Plate 49 (Supposed Self-portrait of young Leonardo)

11. Cartoon for the Virgin and Child with St. Anne and the Infant St. John. Charcoal on brown paper. About 1499. London, Royal Academy

55. *St. John the Baptist.* About 1509–12. Paris, Louvre

56. *Madonna with the Fruit-Plate*. Silverpoint, pen and ink, and wash. About 1481. Paris, Louvre

57. *Madonna Benois*. About 1478–80. Leningrad, Hermitage

*58. Study for the background of the *Adoration of the Kings* (Plate 49). Pen and ink over silverpoint. About 1481. Florence, Uffizi

59. *The Annunciation.* About 1472. Florence, Uffizi

60. Detail from Plate 59

61. Detail from Plate 59

62. Detail from Plate 59

63. Attributed to Leonardo: *Madonna with the Carnation*. About 1478. Munich, Ältere Pinakothek

64. *Madonna of the Rocks*. About 1483–85. Paris, Louvre

65. *Madonna of the Rocks*, About 1506–08. London, National Gallery

*66. *Study for the Head of the Madonna Litta* (Plate 67). Silverpoint on green prepared paper. About 1484. Paris, Louvre

67. Workshop of Leonardo: *Madonna Litta*. About 1485–90. Leningrad, Hermitage

68. *Virgin and Child with St. Anne*. Unfinished. About 1508–10. Paris, Louvre

69. Detail from Plate 68

*70. *Studies for an Adoration of the Child*. Pen and ink over lead point. About 1483. New York, Metropolitan Museum

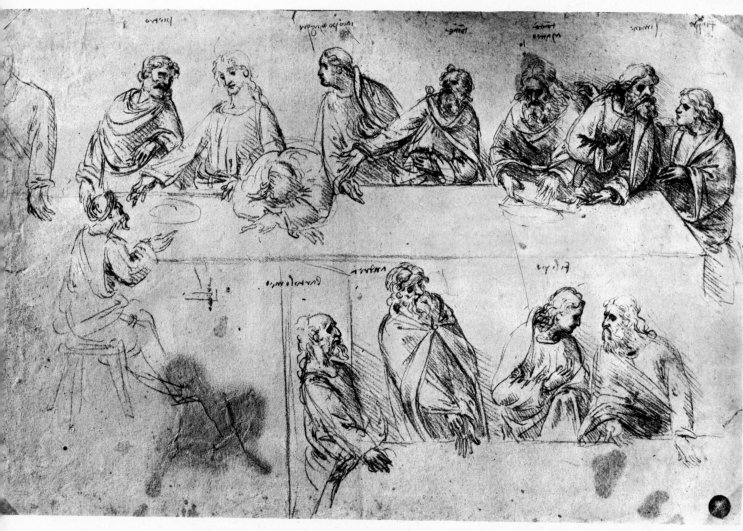

71. *Sketch for* The Last Supper. Red chalk. About 1495. Venice, Academy

72. Reconstruction of the above composition

73. *The Last Supper*. Wall-painting in oil tempera. 1495–98. Milan, Santa Maria delle Grazie

74. Detail from Plate 73

75. Detail from Plate 73

76. *St. Jerome*. Unfinished. About 1483. Rome, Vatican Gallery

77. *Rocky Landscape.* Detail from Plate 76

78. *Rocky Landscape*. Detail from Plate 64

79. *Rocky Landscape*. Detail from Plate 68

*80. *Ravine with Water Birds*. Pen and ink on pinkish paper. About 1478–80. Windsor Castle, Royal Library

Leonardo

*81. *Arno Landscape*. Pen and ink. 1473. Florence, Uffizi

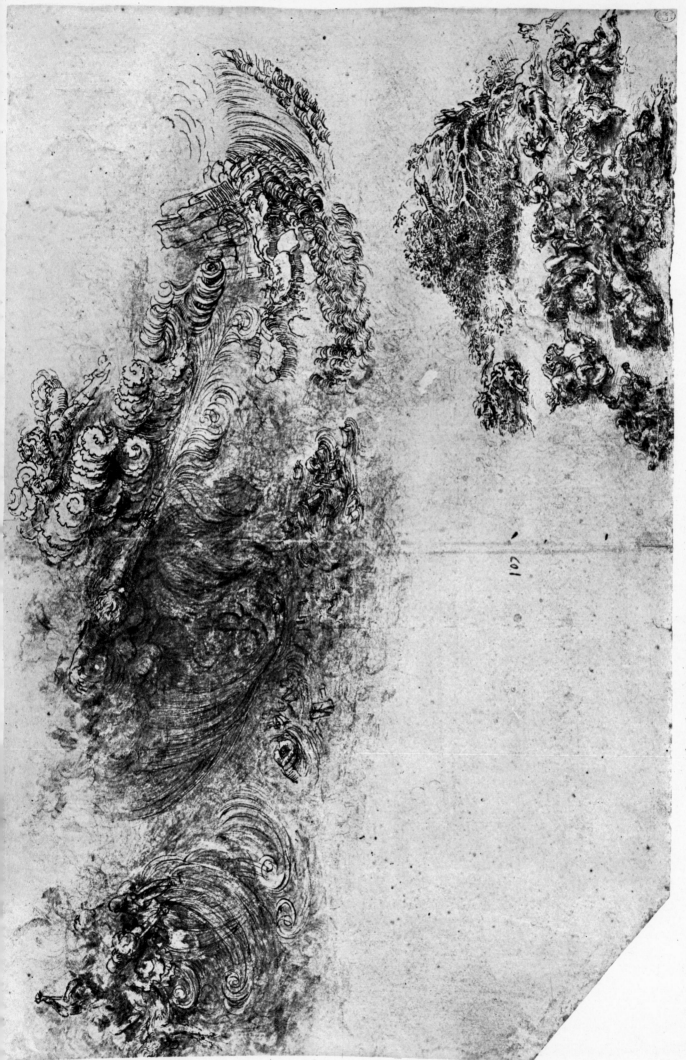

*82. *The Deluge*. Black chalk on grey paper. About 1512–14. Windsor Castle, Royal Library

·137·

*83. *Storm in the Alps*. Red chalk. About 1500. Windsor Castle, Royal Library

*84. *The Ferry*. Pen and ink on yellowish paper. About 1503. Windsor Castle, Royal Library

*85. *The Deluge*. Pen and ink and brown wash over black chalk. About 1514–16. Windsor Castle, Royal Library

86. *Landscape*. Detail from Plate 59

87. *Landscape*. About 1473. (Contributed by Leonardo to Verrocchio's *Baptism of Christ*.) Florence, Uffizi

88. *Plant Ornament*. About 1474–78. On the reverse of the *Portrait of a Lady* in the Liechtenstein Gallery (Plate 23)

89. *Fruit Garlands*. About 1498. Detail from the left lunette over the *Last Supper* (Plate 73). Milan, Santa Maria delle Grazie

90. *Plants*. About 1483. Detail from the *Madonna of the Rocks* (Plate 64). Paris, Louvre

91. *Flowering Plants*. Pen and ink over red chalk. About 1506. Windsor Castle, Royal Library

*92. *Anemones*. Pen and ink. About 1506. Windsor Castle, Royal Library

*93. *Studies of Flowers.* Pen and ink over metal-point, on brownish paper. About 1483. Venice, Academy

94. *Lilies*. Pen and ink and sepia wash, over black chalk. About 1479. Windsor Castle, Royal Library

95. *Undergrowth.* About 1506–08. Detail from the *Madonna of the Rocks* (Plate 65). London, National Gallery

*96. *Flowering Rushes*. Red chalk. About 1504. Windsor Castle, Royal Library

*97. *Oak Leaves with Acorns, and a Spray of Greenweed.* Red chalk, with touches of white, on pink paper. About 1506.
Windsor Castle, Royal Library

98. *Flowering Meadow*. About 1472. Detail from the *Annunciation* (Plate 59). Florence, Uffizi

99. *Irises and Wood Anemones*. About 1483. Detail from the *Madonna of the Rocks* (Plate 64). Paris, Louvre

*100. *A Dog*. Two sketches in red chalk. About 1498. Windsor Castle, Royal Library

*101. *A Bear*. Silverpoint sketches on pinkish buff prepared paper. About 1480–1482. New York, Lehman Collection

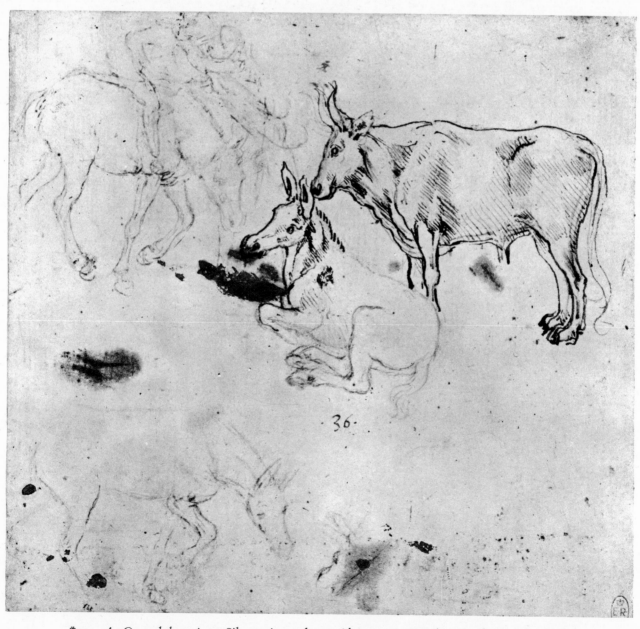

*102. *An Ox and three Asses*. Silverpoint and pen. About 1480. Windsor Castle, Royal Library

103. *Fighting Horsemen*. About 1481–1482. (Detail from Plate 49.) Florence, Uffizi

104. *Dragon Fight*. Pen and wash. About 1482. London, British Museum

105. *Studies of a Dragon Fight*. Pen and ink. About 1506. Windsor Castle, Royal Library

*106. *Study for the Sforza Monument.* Silverpoint on blue prepared paper. About 1488–1490. Windsor Castle, Royal Library

*107. *Studies of Horses' Feet*. Silverpoint on blue prepared paper, heightened with white. About 1490. Turin, Royal Library

108. *The Fight for the Standard.* Copy by Rubens of the centre part of Leonardo's wall painting *The Battle of Anghiari.*
The Hague, Royal Collection

109–110. *Sketches for The Battle of Anghiari.* Pen and ink. About 1503. Venice, Academy

*111. *Studies for the Trivulzio Monument.* Pen sketches on grey paper. About 1511. Windsor Castle, Royal Library

*112. *Studies of Horses*. Silverpoint on blue prepared paper. About 1490. Windsor Castle, Royal Library

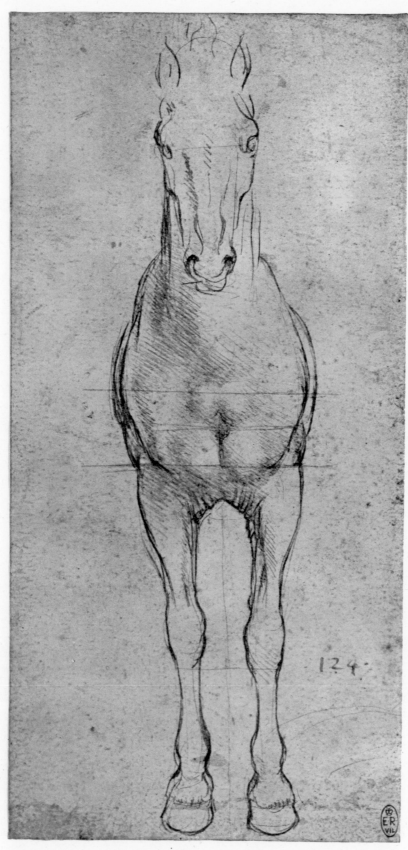

*113. *Study of a Horse*. Silverpoint on blue prepared paper. About 1490.
Windsor Castle, Royal Library

114. Leonardo's Workshop: *Horse and Rider*. Bronze statuette, perhaps after a wax model by the master of about 1506. Budapest, Museum of Fine Arts

NOTES ON THE PLATES

The full titles of books, quoted in abbreviated form in the
Notes on the Plates, can be found in the 'Bibliography'.

Plates marked with an asterisk are reproduced in the original size;
therefore their measurements are not given in the following notes.

Supposed Portraits of Leonardo da Vinci. (a) Leonardo as the supposed model for St Michael. Detail from *Tobias and the three Archangels,* painted in about 1467–70 in Verrocchio's workshop, attributed to (his assistant) Francesco Botticini (Florence, Uffizi). – (b) Leonardo as the supposed model for David. Detail from Verrocchio's bronze statue, about 1473 (Florence, Museo Nazionale). – (c) Bust of an old Man, pen and ink drawing by Leonardo, supposed self-portrait of about 1514. (Amsterdam, Fodor Museum). – (d) Pen and ink drawing by Leonardo, about 1496. This sketch, showing the proportions of the head, was supposed to have been done in front of a mirror (Turin, Library). – (e) Pen and ink drawing by Michelangelo, about 1503, supposed portrait of Leonardo lecturing on anatomy (London, British Museum). – (f) Supposed portrait of Leonardo as Plato. Detail from Raphael's *School of Athens,* 1509–11 (Rome, Vatican). – (g) King David, Detail from Raphael's *Disputa Del Sacramento,* 1509–11 (Rome, Vatican).

1

SELF-PORTRAIT. Turin, 15571

According to Berenson (1083), retouched on nostrils and mouth. 33.3×21.4 cm.

The illustrations on p. 150 indicate the various opinions held on the appearance of Leonardo. The profile of the woodcut by Cristoforo Coriolano in Vasari's *Life of Leonardo* (p. 9), corresponds with a profile drawing at Windsor Castle (No. 12726, attributed to Ambrogio de Predis). Vasari himself had, in 1557, painted a likeness of Leonardo in the mural in the Palazzo Vecchio at Florence, *Leo X and his Cardinals*. On the other hand, the well-known 'Self-Portrait of Leonardo' in the Uffizi is a fake and the X-ray photographs show that it has been painted over a German picture representing a St Mary Magdalene, datable about 1620.

Berenson, Gronau and Calvi thought they had found a youthful self-portrait of Leonardo in the *Adoration of the Kings* (plate 53). Müller-Walde and Bayersdorfer suspected that Leonardo was the model for the St Michael in Botticini's *Tobias and the Archangels* (fig. a); the same suggestion has been repeatedly put forward for Verrocchio's *David* (fig. b). Beltrami contributed a little to the confusion by his idea that certain sketches of heads with measurements of proportions (e.g. fig. d) were drawn by Leonardo in front of a mirror. Beltrami and Nicodemi maintain that a sketch in Amsterdam (fig. c), representing an old man, or perhaps an Apostle, is simply another self-portrait of the master. (Adolfo Venturi and Valentiner thought that this drawing was freely copied by Leonardo from Michelangelo's *Moses*, which would date it rather late; Berenson took it for the sketch for a figure in an *Adoration*, which would date it rather early.) Marie Herzfeld and Müntz called a drawing at Windsor, plate 6, a self-portrait of Leonardo. Möller found a portrait of the master in a Michelangelo drawing (fig. e); this figure is of the same type as Raphael's *Plato*, or even his *David* (figs. f and g); and as all the *ciceroni* in Rome will tell you, Raphael's *Plato* is again a portrait of Leonardo!

2

FIVE GROTESQUE HEADS. Windsor, 12495

Sometimes called 'The temperaments'. The inscription on the reverse of the drawing, Richter § 1355. Kenneth Clark: 'This is the most important of all Leonardo's caricature drawings.' Old copies in the Louvre and at Weimar.

3

BUST OF A WARRIOR. British Museum, 1895–9-15-474, from the Malcolm Collection (Cat. 1950, No. 96).

Doubted by Morelli and others, and ascribed to Verrocchio. This drawing is done with the left hand, and it is certainly by Leonardo. It was always thought to be connected with two reliefs, 'Scipio' (or Alexander) and 'Darius', executed in Verrocchio's workshop and sent to Matthias Corvinus of Hungary. Of those two reliefs, as Bode contended, old copies and versions are preserved (*Leonardo-Studien*, p. 28); amongst others the Scipio relief in the Louvre from the Rattier collection, which is sometimes attributed to Leonardo himself (Möller, Valentiner, a.o.); a clay relief of an old warrior in the Berlin Museum, attributed to the Robbia workshop (No. 2014, Sch. 188), and a circular relief, with the same bust of an old warrior, in the Louvre (ill. Müller-Walde, 1889, p. 71). The *Alexander* relief in the Herbert

Workshop of Verrocchio: *Scipio Africanus*. Detail of a marble relief, out 1478. Paris, Louvre (No. 668) from the Rattier Collection.

N. Strauss collection, New York, is an original work by Verrocchio and has generally been accepted as one of the two reliefs sent by Lorenzo Magnifico to Matthias Corvinus. Vasari speaks, however, about '*due teste di metallo*', and as the existing copies of the Darius relief give one rather the feeling that the original has been formed in clay and cast in bronze or silver, one cannot be certain that Vasari has made a mistake about the material.

The assumption is that Leonardo's drawing of an old warrior is freely copied from Verrocchio's *Darius* relief, or else, that it is a design for a similar relief, in imitation of Verrocchio's style. (See Planiscig, *Verrocchio*, Vienna, 1941, plates 36–38.)

Leonardo's warrior is obviously an ideal type similar to Verrocchio's *Colleoni*, and to the warrior in Verrocchio's silver relief of the *Beheading of the Baptist*, from the altar of San Giovanni, now in the Museo del Duomo, Florence. (About Verrocchio as the creator of this style, and about his influence on Leonardo, see Planiscig, pp. 8–10. Compare E. Jacobsen, in *Kunstchronik*, 1906–07, p. 194f.)

Very interesting is the fantastic armour of Leonardo's warrior, the armour *alla romana*. Armour of this kind was certainly produced in Verrocchio's workshop, and a helmet in the Florence Bargello shows the same bat wings, and the same circular ornament on the wings. A Leonardo drawing at Windsor (12370) contains sketches for a highly decorated cuirass, proving how much Leonardo was concerned with the armourer's art during the time he assisted Verrocchio.

4

HEADS OF GIRLS AND MEN. Windsor, 12276 verso. 40.5×29 cm.

Recto of the same sheet contains a Madonna drawing. The youth in the centre closely resembles the Rattier Relief, as Bode observed (see illustration on p. 151). The type of the old man was repeated by Leonardo throughout his life.

5

SKETCHES OF THE HEAD AND SHOULDERS OF A WOMAN. Windsor, 12513

Six of these seventeen studies show the figure seen from the back; therefore they can hardly have been done directly for a Madonna composition; they are just studies of movement.

6

OLD MAN THINKING. Windsor, 12579. 15.2× 21.3 cm.

The sheet is folded in the middle, and contains two separate drawings: the reproduction gives only the left half of the sheet. The right half shows sketches of swirling water and plaited hair, and a note (see Richter § 389).

7

STUDY FOR THE HEAD OF A PHARISEE. Windsor, 19106

Seidlitz thought it a study for the Judas in the *Last Supper* (*Leonardo*, second edition, 1935, p. 150). The sheet is folded in the middle, the left half containing little sketches of twigs and notes on physics; the right half (which alone is reproduced here) the turbanned head. (The two drawings on this folded sheet are not necessarily of the same date.) Kenneth Clark connects this drawing with a (lost) painting, *Christ among the Doctors*, for which Leonardo received a commission, in 1504, from Isabella d'Este of Mantua.

Bernardino Luini: *Christ among the Doctors* (after Leonardo). London, National Gallery.

According to Vasari, Leonardo painted (c. 1513) for Baldassare Turini da Pescia, who was Datary to Pope Leo X '*un fanciuletto, che è bello e grazioso a maraviglia*'. Seidlitz (p. 375) and Heydenreich (p. 201) understand this as a *Head of Christ as a Boy*. Such a Head is in the Museo Lázaro Galdiano, Madrid, attributed there to Leonardo himself, but apparently by the same hand as the *Girl with Cherries* at the Metropolitan Museum, which is now generally attributed to Ambrogio de Predis.

8

CHRIST CARRYING THE CROSS. Venice, 231

This small drawing shows just the head of Christ crowned with thorns, and the hand of a beadle clutching the hair. It seems feasible that of this composition Leonardo executed not only one but two cartoons, which are lost and now known only by different imitations.

In the first cartoon Christ was turned to the left (as in

Christ carrying the Cross. Fresco by Sodoma, 1506–08.
Monteoliveto Maggiore.

Christ carrying the Cross. Attributed to Giorgione, about
1506. Boston, Isabella Stewart Gardner Museum.

the drawing), and I imagine that Leonardo took this cartoon with him to Venice, as all imitations I know of this version belong to the Venetian School.[1] I reproduce here the one which originated in the workshop of Giovanni Bellini, and of which at least three copies are extant; the best of the three, though the least Bellinesque, is thought to be a copy by Giorgione (though Philip Hendy ascribed it to Palma Vecchio).

In the other, and later, version Christ was turned to the right, and this composition was imitated only by Milanese painters. The most beautiful of these adaptations is Sodoma's fresco in the convent of Monteoliveto Maggiore.

Charles Loeser (1903) called the attribution of this drawing (plate 8) to Leonardo a 'defamation'.

9

HEAD OF CHRIST. Brera, 280. 40×32 cm.
This drawing, a study for the Christ of *The Last Supper* (plate 74), is in the worst state possible, half destroyed and overpainted with chalks, and tempera, but it still retains its magic. I think it gives a much better idea of how the head of Christ in *The Last Supper* looked

1. Leonardo was in Venice in the spring of 1500, the only sojourn of which we have documentary evidence. This happened when he travelled from Milan to Florence. When, in 1506, he travelled from Florence to Milan, he could have visited Venice again; at least, his influence on the art of Bellini and Giorgione is most apparent about this time.

originally than what is left of it in the wall-painting itself (plate 74). It has been doubted, of course, many times, e.g. by G. Carotti, who ascribed it to Cesare da Sesto; and it has been zealously defended, e.g. by Prof. Hildebrandt (in his *Leonardo*, 1927, pp. 98–101; see also Sirén, 1916, p. 109).

It is the ghost of a Leonardo drawing; worse still, it is a rouged and made-up ghost; but it remains the only visible thing we can take hold of if we want to dream how Leonardo painted the central figure of his masterpiece.

There are two notes by Leonardo which prove that he made studies from living persons, meaning to use their features as a model for the figure of Christ in *The Last Supper*. One of the notes reads, 'Christ. Count Giovanni, the one with the Cardinal of Mortaro' (S.K. M. II–1, 3a). The other, 'Alessandro Carissimo of Parma, for the hand of Christ' (same note-book, 6a).

According to Vasari (1568) and Francesco Bocchi (1584), Leonardo left the head of Christ in the wall-painting unfinished.

10 and 11

STUDIES FOR THE HEAD OF LEDA.
Windsor, 12516 and 12518
Leonardo made two different cartoons for a Leda painting, one for a Leda with the Swan in a crouching position, and one for a standing Leda. (Cf. notes on plates 36 and 37.) The latter was copied by Raphael

during his stay at Florence, about 1506, in a pen and ink drawing which is now at Windsor Castle.

A sketch in oil, from Leonardo's studio, of a similar head was in Lord Melchett's possession, a repetition is in the Parma Gallery, and other copies in the William van Horne Collection, Montreal, and in the Johnson Collection, Philadelphia. Those four versions are painted on wooden panels. A much better brush drawing in umbra on linen, similar in technique to Leonardo's drapery studies on canvas, is in the Pietro del Giudice Collection, London.

12 and 13

HEADS OF WARRIORS. Budapest, Museum of Fine Arts, Nos. 344 and 343.

Studies for the helmeted figure on the right, and for the two central figures in the cartoon for the *Battle of Anghiari*. See plate 108. On the reverse of No. 12 is a sketch in metal-point, a helmeted man carrying a lance over his left shoulder; a rather weak drawing. According to Suida (p. 142), No. 12, and perhaps also No. 13, are only copies; but neither Popham (1946), nor Heydenreich (1954), nor Kenneth Clark (1958) have agreed to this condemnation of the two particularly fine drawings.

14

STUDY OF AN APOSTLE. Vienna, Albertina, Cat. No. III, 18.

Pen over metal-point; some of the ink lines are perhaps by a later hand.

Usually regarded as a study for St Peter (plate 73, the head between Judas and St John), which is difficult to accept. It is probably a study for the Apostle Simeon in the first version of *The Last Supper* – see the second figure from the right in the upper row of plate 71.

15–17

STUDIES FOR HEADS OF APOSTLES IN THE LAST SUPPER. Windsor, 12552, 12548 and 12557.

For St James the Greater (No. 15) compare the head at the extreme right in plate 74; for St Bartholomew (No. 16) the head at the extreme left in plate 73; for St Philip (No. 17) the head at the extreme right in plate 75.

18

HEAD OF ST ANNE. Windsor, 12534

Study for the cartoon of St Anne, which Fra Pietro da Novellara described in 1501 (see Document XI, on p. 37). See also the note to plate 54. The face in the drawing much retouched by a later hand.

19

HEAD OF A YOUNG WOMAN. Windsor, 12512. 16.5×12.4 cm.

According to Kenneth Clark, 'the silver-point outline of the back of the head, neck, bust, etc., is so masterly and has so much Leonardo's rhythm of hand that we are tempted to say that the drawing originally was by him, and has been worked over by a pupil.' Some of the shading, although very little of it, is from left to right. This drawing appears to me a very important example of a workshop production, where a sketch by the master was made into a finished drawing by one of his pupils – perhaps by Ambrogio de Predis. Compare the cartoon, plate 24, which is also worked over by a pupil.

20

STUDY FOR THE ANGEL'S HEAD IN THE VIRGIN OF THE ROCKS. Turin, 15572
Cf. plates 21 and 64.

21

ANGEL'S HEAD. Detail from plate 64, Madonna of the Rocks, Paris, Louvre. (The reproduction is in original size.)

22

LADY WITH AN ERMINE. Cracow, No. 180. Panel, 55×40.4 cm.

In ancient times ermines (Greek, *galé*) were kept as mouse-hunters instead of cats.[2] This also appears to have been sometimes a custom in the Renaissance, as a big weasel is depicted in this portrait, and a small one in a lady's portrait from Titian's studio (Vienna Museum, and a variant in the John Ringling Art Museum, Sarasota, U.S.A.).

Leonardo used the ermine, or *galé*, as a speaking symbol in this portrait of Cecilia Gallerani, as he used the juniper, or *ginevra*, in the portrait of Ginevra de'Benci; a cock, or *gallo*, in the allegory on Gian Galeazzo Sforza; and the knots, the *fantasie dei vinci*, as a symbol for his own name.

2. 'Professor Rolleston and others believed that the domestic animal of the Greeks and Romans, for which we now use the cat, was the white-breasted marten. The word *felis*, it is true, is commonly used for the weasel' (Watkins, *Natural History of the Ancients*, London, 1896, p. 63). Bode (*Leonardo-Studien*, p. 112) thought that Leonardo was depicting a marten, or rather a ferret (Mustela furo), as he never saw a real ermine. (See also G. Jennison, *Animals in Ancient Rome*, 1937, pp. 19 and 129.) The ermine was also the emblem of Ludovico Sforza.

Cecilia Gallerani became the mistress of Ludovico Moro in 1481, and the portrait was painted shortly after Leonardo arrived in Milan.

The ermine is the best part of the picture, as the critics, including Ochenkowski, Hildebrandt and Clark, are all agreed. Otherwise, the painting is not well preserved. The lower part of the hand has been repainted as well as the left shoulder and the part of the dress underneath the ermine, where Cecilia's left hand was originally sketched in. The dark background is new, and the outline of the figure spoilt by it. New also is the inscription in the upper left corner: 'La belle Feroniere Leonard d'Awinci,' which suggests that the picture had been in France before it came into the possession of Prince Adam Czartoryski during the French Revolution.

In spite of its doubtful preservation, this is Leonardo's most charming portrait painting. Seidlitz attributed this portrait to Ambrogio de Predis, Gronau and Sirén to Boltraffio. Berenson, Kenneth Clark, and Heydenreich give it to Leonardo, which is indeed correct.

23

PORTRAIT OF GINEVRA DE' BENCI. Vaduz, Liechtenstein Gallery, 32. Panel, 42×37 cm.

On the reverse a sprig of juniper encircled by laurel and palm forming a garland, with the inscription 'virtutem forma decorat' (plate 88). The garland, in its mutilated shape, on the back of the panel proves that the painting has been cut by c. 8 inches; the lower part, originally containing the hands, is lost. The slit of the bodice has been overpainted; originally the fingers of the right hand, probably holding some flowers, were painted here. A drawing at Windsor (plate 33) might have been a study for the hands of this portrait.[3]

Juniper (ginepro or ginevra in Italian) is the symbol for the name of the sitter. The Libro di Antonio Billi (c. 1518), the Anonimo Gaddiano (c. 1542) and also Vasari (1550 and 1568) confirm that Leonardo portrayed Ginevra de' Benci, and they praise the picture. The Anonimo says: 'Ritrasse in Firenze al naturale la Ginevra d' Amerigo Benci, la quale tanto bene finì, che non il ritratto ma la propria Ginevra pareva'. (See p. 31.)

24

PORTRAIT OF ISABELLA D'ESTE. Louvre, M.I. 753. (The reproduction is reduced to two-thirds of the original size.)

3. Why has the lower part of the painting been cut off? No one painted hands more beautifully than Leonardo did. I suspect that the painting was unfinished, the hands only sketched in (as the left hand of the Lady with the Ermine, or the right hand of the Musician, plates 22 and 26). Ginevra was born in 1456, in 1473 she married Luigi Niccolini, in 1490 she was still alive.

The drawing is pricked for transfer, but the painting done from it is lost. Leonardo painted Isabella in 1500 – see Documents IX and X. There were at least two portraits of Isabella, one which Leonardo left in Mantua (and which probably was later in Fontainebleau) and one which he had with him in Venice, as we know from a letter from Lorenzo Gusnasco to Isabella d'Este, dated March 13th, 1500. And it may be that Leonardo painted a third 'sketch', fulfilling Isabella's wish.

The cartoon reproduced here is of very poor preservation.[4] The reproduction gives only a part of the drawing, as the head only is by Leonardo, and the dress and hand by a mediocre pupil, who unfortunately was bold enough to redraw even the profile. The cartoon must have been famous, because there are several old copies of it, including one at Oxford, showing the hands in the right position resting on a book, and one at the Uffizi, the head only, probably by Ambrogio de Predis. Other copies are in the Munich Print-room, and in the British Museum.

25

PORTRAIT OF A GIRL. Windsor, 12505. 32×20 cm.

Chin and other parts of the face re-drawn, but probably by Leonardo himself.

26

PORTRAIT OF A MUSICIAN. Ambrosiana, sala E.19. Panel, 43×31 cm.

In Leonardo's List of Drawings (Richter § 680) of c. 1482 there is one item: 'una testa ritratta d'Atalanta che alzava il volto.' This probably means that Leonardo portrayed the musician Atalanta Migliorotti, who had learned from him to play the lyre (according to the Anonimo Gaddiano) and who went with him from Florence to Milan in 1482. Atalanta moved in 1490 to Mantua; and in 1513, when Leonardo came to Rome, he found Atalanta there as Superintendent of the buildings of Pope Leo X.

Nevertheless, Luca Beltrami, who saw in the Ambrosiana picture a portrait of Franchino Gaffurio, was probably right. In 1905, the picture was freed from overpaint, and the sheet was revealed with music notes and a half-effaced inscription line on it, reading CANT ... ANG ... Now Gaffurio, conductor of the Cathedral choir in Milan from 1483, was the author of an

4. Popham, p. 120: 'Of the authenticity of this it is difficult to speak; in its present state one cannot say that it represents much of the master's handiwork'. Nevertheless, he reproduces this important cartoon (fig. 172).

Franchino Gaffurio, playing the organ. Woodcut (detail) from his *Angelicum ac divinum opus musicae*, Milan, 1508. (This block was first used in 1480.)

Franchino Gaffurio, teaching the theory of music. Woodcut from his *De harmonia musicae disciplinae*, 1480. (Inscribed: *Harmonia est discordiæ concors*.)

'Angelicum ac divinum opus', not published until 1508, but composed probably much earlier.[5] We may read the inscription on the sheet in the Ambrosiana musician's hand as 'canticum angelicum', which would be the title of a work by Gaffurio. According to Gerolamo Adda, Leonardo made the designs for the woodcuts in Gaffurio's 'Practica musicae', published at Milan, 1496. Gaffurio, born 1451, was of about the same age as Leonardo.

As a third possibility, the inscription could be read CANT(or) ANG(elo), which would make it a portrait of Angelo Testagrossa, who in 1496 was the singing-master of Isabella d'Este.[6]

This portrait is the only painting by Leonardo which is in a perfect state of preservation. Only the face and a part of the hair are finished; everything else, including the hand, is just sketched in. All the brush strokes, especially those on the cheek-bone and the neck, seem to me to be made by a left-handed painter. For the rather strange design of the eyes, compare the drawing of an angel, from the same period, plate 20.[7]

5. The woodcut representations of Gaffurio do not contradict the identification of this picture as a portrait of him. The woodcut from *De harmonia musicae* was first published in 1480; the other from *Angelicum ac divinum opus* was also first printed at Naples in 1480, and reprinted at Milan in 1492 and 1508. (See A. M. Hind, *History of Woodcut*, 1935, vol. I, p. 516.)

6. I am mentioning this although I am convinced that this is a portrait of Franchino Gaffurio, and of no one else.

7. Adolfo Venturi (1941) followed Morelli and Seidlitz in attributing this portrait to Ambrogio de Predis. A similar portrait in the Ambrosiana, Milan (inscribed '*vita si scias uti longa est*'), certainly a work of Ambrogio de Predis, shows the inferiority of the pupil's art.

27

PORTRAIT OF A YOUNG LADY IN PRO-FILE. Ambrosiana, sala E, 8. Panel, 51×34 cm.
Müller-Walde thought it a portrait of Bianca, a natural daughter of Ludovico Moro, for which painting Leonardo received a commission in 1491. Bode, Gronau and Beltrami[8] attributed it without any reservation to Leonardo; Suida thinks that Leonardo did the better part of the portrait; Kenneth Clark suggested that the master may have painted some of the details, especially the headdress.[9] But Morelli, Berenson, Bodmer, Sirén and other experts regard it as the master-piece of Ambrogio de Predis. R. Longhi is alone in attributing it to Lorenzo Costa (*Ampliamenti nell' officina Ferrarese*, 1940, p. 142).

I believe that it was designed by Leonardo in his work-shop but not executed by him. Ambrogio de Predis is certainly responsible for some of the weaknesses of the painting, mainly for the insensitive, dark background, by which he even spoiled the outlines of the back of the head and the shoulder.[10] The flesh is much better

8. Luca Beltrami, *Leonardo e i disfattisti suoi*, Milan, 1919, p. 64 f.

9. May we assume that Leonardo designed, for the Court jeweller, jewellery as worn by the Lady of this portrait? The golden *ghirlanda* or *ferronnière* round the brow, the net made of gold wire and pearls, and the interlaced wire ornament over the shoulder are of exquisite design. An engraving by Jaques Prévost de Gray, a portrait of Francis I (Bibl. Nat., Paris, reprod. Bouchot, *Pièces choisies de l'école Française*), shows the King with a neck-chain formed of shells and *fantasie dei vinci*, which looks as if designed by Leonardo.

10. From 1796 to 1815 the picture was in Paris where, apparently, it was restored. There are several pictures at the Louvre showing the same poor style of restoration.

modelled, softer and more lifelike than anything Predis ever painted, including the Archinto portrait with its sooty shadows in the National Gallery, dated 1494 (which is most probably by him), or the utterly disagreeable profile of Emperor Maximilian in the Vienna Museum, dated 1502.

Profile portraits by Leonardo are scarce; but compare, for example, plate 25; or plate 24; or the portraits of Ludovico Sforza and his family, plate 11: which all belong to the 1490's.

28, 29

MONA LISA. Louvre, No. 1601. Panel, 77×53 cm. The only Leonardo portrait painting which has never been questioned. The sitter was Lisa Gherardini, born in 1479, married in 1495 to Francesco di Zanobi del Giocondo of Florence. Leonardo brought the painting to France (see Document XVI), where Francis I bought it for 12,000 francs.

The preservation of the painting is not too good; there are overpaintings in the dress, the veil, the right hand, in the sky and elsewhere. Part of the glazes is rubbed off, and the whole is covered by dirty greenish varnish. According to Wölfflin (Seidlitz, 1935, p. 268) the dress was originally green and the sleeves yellow. The picture is cut both sides, about 3 inches.[11]

The cleaning of the picture has often been considered, but the French artists, especially Degas, protested against it; and they were right.

Many pages have been written since Vasari's time on the 'Smile of the Gioconda'. A Frenchman (Robert de Sizeranne, 1896) has observed that Gioconda smiles with only the left part of her mouth – but this is in accordance with the advice given to women in Renaissance times as to how to look most graceful: we read in Agnolo Firenzuola's 'Della perfetta bellezza d'una donna', 1541: 'From time to time, to close the mouth at the right corner with a suave and nimble movement, and to open it at the left side, as if you were smiling secretly . . . not in an artificial manner, but as though unconsciously – this is not affectation, if it is done in moderation and in a restrained and graceful manner and accompanied by innocent coquetry and by certain movements of the eyes. . . .' This is a precept for ladies of fashion, and we should not overlook the fact that Mona Lisa – who plucked her eye-brows and the hair above her brow – was one of them.[12]

11. Concerning the state of preservation of the Leonardo paintings in the Louvre see C. Wolters, in *Kunstchronik*, 1952, p. 135 f.

12. Vasari describes Mona Lisa's eye-brows indeed in detail. Did he mean the eye-lashes? The excellent Milanese restorer Cavenaghi stated (Seidlitz, p. 509) that eye-brows have never been painted in this portrait.

[The *Mona Lisa* is probably the most popular portrait in the world. And its popularity was considerably enhanced when thirty years ago it was stolen from the Louvre and remained undiscovered for more than two years. The thief was an Italian house-painter, Vincenzo Peruggia, who did occasional work at the Louvre. On the 21st of August, 1911, at 8 o'clock in the morning he took the picture out of its frame, put it under his workman's blouse, marched through a backdoor and down to the quay. He was questioned by the Police, but they did not find the painting which he kept in a small storeroom at his lodgings. When two years later, in Florence, Peruggia offered the smiling Gioconda to an art-dealer, Alfred Gori by name, he was arrested, and the picture was surrendered to the French Ambassador on the 21st December, 1913. Peruggia declared he had taken this Italian picture to Italy, being himself a Lombard and a patriot. He was sentenced to seven months imprisonment.]

30

THE PROPORTIONS OF THE HUMAN FIGURE. Venice, 228. 34.3×24.5 cm. (A part of the text underneath the figure is not reproduced here.) This drawing is an illustration to a passage in Vitruvius, book III, cap. 1 (Richter § 343), and Leonardo's writing on the sheet is a free rendering of what Vitruvius said; but Leonardo did not copy the sentences which he in fact illustrated, viz.: 'The navel is naturally placed in the centre of the human body, and if a circle be described of a man lying with his face upward and his hands and feet extended, it will touch his fingers and his toes. It is not alone by a circle that the human body is thus circumscribed, as may be seen by placing it within a square. For if we measure from the feet to the crown of the head, and then across the arms fully extended, we should find the latter measure equal to the former; so that the lines at right angles to each other enclosing the figure, would form a square.'

31

NUDE FIGURE OF A MAN, HIS BACK TURNED TO THE SPECTATOR. Windsor, 12596 Probably done in connection with the earliest studies for the Battle of Anghiari.

32

STUDIES OF HANDS. Windsor, 12616 For the *Adoration of the Kings*, Uffizi (1481, plate 49). The sheet is partly discoloured by damp and the fine silver-point lines are hardly visible on the pink preparation; this reproduction is based on a ultra-violet photograph which shows much more than one can see in the original drawing. (See Popham, in *Burlington Magazine*, XCIV, pp. 127–132.)

33

STUDY OF A WOMAN'S HANDS. Windsor, 12558

See the note on plate 23: the drawing has been connected (by Müller-Walde) with the Ginevra portrait in the Liechtenstein Gallery, and with Verrocchio's marble bust of a *Lady with Primulas* (Florence, Museo Nazionale, attributed to Leonardo by Mackowsky, Bode, and, with some reservation, by Suida); see the illustration on p. 25.

34

POINTING WOMAN IN A LANDSCAPE, NEAR A WATERFALL. Windsor, 12581

This drawing, probably done during Leonardo's late period in Rome and under the influence of Hellenistic reliefs, also shows how far Leonardo had returned to the style of his native Florence; Seidlitz (p. 215) felt reminded of Botticelli.

The landscape – with the little waterfall in the left corner, the trees on both sides, the river, and the hills disappearing in the distance as in a grey haze – is barely indicated, but is as full of atmosphere as any late drawing by Rembrandt.

This drawing is dated sometimes too early (Seidlitz: c. 1491) and sometimes too late (Heydenreich: one of the last drawings). The technique of the drawing is the same as in the study for the Trivulzio monument, Windsor, No. 12354, of about 1511, and the Deluge series, Windsor, e.g. No. 12383, of about 1514. The *Pointing Woman* is later than No. 12354, and earlier than 12383.

35

YOUTH IN MASQUERADE COSTUME. Windsor, 12575

Malaguzzi Valeri, Seidlitz and Bodmer dated this drawing early, connecting it with a masquerade for Count Galeazzo Sanseverino, in 1491; Müller-Walde thought it was done in the first Florentine period, for the joust of Giuliano de' Medici in 1475. Calvi attributed it to the later Milan period. Popp attributed it to the French period, 1517–18, and Heydenreich accepted this date. Sir Kenneth Clark thought the drawing should be dated after 1513. Thus, the main problem of this drawing is its date.

In May, 1506, Leonardo was summoned to Milan by the Governor, Charles d'Amboise; he obtained three months' leave from the Signoria of Florence, and in September of that year the leave was prolonged, without the Signoria's consent. He stayed another full year in Milan, and he suspended his work on the painting of the Battle of Anghiari in the Sala di Gran Consiglio, and never resumed it. Why was Leonardo summoned to Milan? Certainly he would not have been granted leave merely to put the last touches to an altar-piece for an obscure monastery. I think this leave was granted because Louis XII was expected in Milan, who actually entered the town on the 23rd May, 1507, when three triumphal arches were erected in his honour and two hundred youths in costumes of blue silk welcomed him.[13] I imagine Leonardo's masquerade drawings (Windsor, 12573–77) were done in this year.

All Leonardo's late drawings are marked by a profound *tristesse* and exhibit a dissolution of form which recall the later Titian and Rembrandt. I cannot discern the same spirit in those lively and plastic costume drawings which continue the style of the drawings for the St Anne cartoon, but are earlier than those for the Trivulzio monument. I should not date any of the Windsor drawings 12573–77 later than 1507.

36

LEDA AND THE SWAN. Chatsworth, 717

A sketch in the Codex Atlanticus (289 recto), datable c. 1504, three small sketches at Windsor (12337), a drawing at Chatsworth, a drawing at Rotterdam (formerly at Weimar), an unpleasing painting once at Castle Neuwied (usually ascribed to Gianpetrino) – that is all that is left of Leonardo's composition of a kneeling Leda. The mother of Castor and Pollux, of Clytemnestra and Helen, appears in this drawing sharply differentiated from the slender Venus of Botticelli, the tall figure of Eve as the Florentines drew her since Ghiberti, or even Raphael's Three Graces: it is a baroque type of a woman, fleshy, like a mare: fertility symbolized by heavy curves. This Leda is the re-born Bathing Venus of the Greek Baroque and the forerunner of the fat beauties of Rubens.

Morelli attributed this, and the drawing at Rotterdam, to Sodoma; Seidlitz thought that they were only copies after Leonardo. Kenneth Clark believes that the Chatsworth drawing may be a copy. But both drawings were accepted as genuine by Berenson, Suida, Giglioli, Heydenreich, and others, and are now almost generally regarded as autographs. They are certainly both from the same hand, and both not free from retouches.

13. In Luca Landucci's *Florentine Diary* there is a note under the 23rd May, 1507: 'The King of France entered Milan, and there were jousts and feasts'. Isabella d'Este was present. (Marie Herzfeld's edition of Landucci's diary, 1913, vol. II, p. 139 f.)

Leda. Pen and ink over black chalk, by Leonardo, about 1504. Windsor (12337 r., detail, enlarged).

Leda and the Swan. Pen and ink over black chalk, by Leonardo, about 1504, Rotterdam, Boymans Museum (Koenigs Collection).

In the present drawing the body of Leda was at first much thinner; parts were added from the armpits to the hips, and now both shoulders appear to be wrongly attached. The composition has a triangular shape, a pattern followed by Raphael in his Esterházy Madonna, which dates from the same time, about 1504. In the Rotterdam version (which, I believe, is earlier than the one at Chatsworth) the head of Leda is turned to look at the swan, and the swan is lowered and made heavier, appearing like a phallic symbol. The painted version formerly at Castle Neuwied is badly composed and has probably very little to do with any Leonardo design; but, of course, Gianpetrino was at all times *imitating* Leonardo. (The two very interesting Leda engravings by the 'Master I. B. with the Bird', on the other hand, produced probably in about 1500 or a few years later, are completely independent.)

A tiny sketch for the *Standing Leda* is stuck on the *verso* of the sheet 12642 at Windsor. Heydenreich, however, suggested tentatively that this sketch could be for a *Venus* by Leonardo, mentioned by Amoretti. (Seidlitz, 1935, p. 337; Heydenreich, 1954, p. 203.) A similar sketch for a *Standing Leda* is fol. 156 *recto* of the Codex Atlanticus. This figure has been used in a painting *Venus and Amor* by Beccafumi (Leonardo Exhibition at Los Angeles,

1949, No. 69), now in the Isaac Delgado Museum, New Orleans.

37

LEDA AND THE SWAN. Free copy of a lost Leonardo painting of about 1506. Rome, Collection of Contessa Gallotti Spiridon. (Formerly Coll. Comtesse de Rozière, Paris; Baronne de Ruble, Paris. – See Lionello Venturi, *Catalogo della Collezione Ludovico Spiridon*, Amsterdam, 1932.) Panel, 114×86 cm.

This composition is derived from the later version of the *Kneeling Leda* (plate 36): the heads of woman and bird are in the same direction. The right arm of Leda is stretched across her body, as in the sketch of the *Kneeling Leda* at Windsor (12337).

Raphael made a copy in pen and ink from Leonardo's cartoon (Windsor 12759), presumably during his stay in Florence (1504–08).[14]

14. This is far from being certain. Seidlitz (1935, p. 335), following Morelli, attributes this rather poor drawing to Sodoma and thinks that it was 'certainly' done by him in Milan after 1508. Gronau, Fischel, Kenneth Clark, Heydenreich, and Popham, on the other hand regard it as an authentic drawing by Raphael, datable 1505–08. Professor Amadore Porcella, who thinks that the Spiridon picture is an original work by Leonardo, painted in Rome (1514–16), assumes that Raphael copied it there and so late.

Leonardo's *Leda* is mentioned by the Anonimo Gaddiano, although in a doubtful way (see footnote 16 on p. 31). The reference is crossed out and replaced by a reference to the (now lost) cartoon of *Adam and Eve*. It may be that the *Leda* mentioned by the Anonimo in c. 1542, was a cartoon, in some ways resembling the *Adam and Eve* cartoon, not only because both contained a large number of plants but perhaps also alike in the movement of the female figure.

Lomazzo (1584 and 1590) gave some description of Leonardo's *Leda*: '*Facendo Leda tutta ignuda col cigno in grembo, che vergognosamente abassa gli occhi.*'[15]

According to Lomazzo this painting (or cartoon?) went to France and was in the possession of Francis I. The *Leda* which Cassiano del Pozzo saw in 1625 at the Palais de Fontainebleau was doubtless a painting; he describes it as a standing figure of Leda almost entirely naked, well finished but somewhat dry in style, consisting of three long panels which had broken apart, causing a certain loss of paint.

Père Dan, who in 1642 made a list of the pictures at Fontainebleau, does not mention Leonardo's *Leda*; but the name of the picture appears again, and for the last time, in a Fontainebleau Inventory of 1694.[16]

In 1722 a Leda cartoon was seen at Milan in the collection of Marchese Casnedi by Edward Wright (*Some observations made in travelling through France and Italy in the years 1720 and 1722*, London, 1730, p. 471.) According to Langton Douglas (pp. 37–41) the Casnedi collection of cartoons, including a St Anne cartoon, can be traced back to Melzi's heritage, which means the drawings, cartoons, paintings and manuscripts left to Francesco Melzi by Leonardo in his Will. The St Anne cartoon from the Casnedi collection is now in the Royal Academy, London, the Leda cartoon is missing.

15. 'Entirely nude, with the swan in her lap, and her eyes bashfully cast down.' This description does not quite agree with the known copies of the *Standing Leda*; *in grembo* can hardly mean 'in her arms'. Adolf Rosenberg (*Leonardo*, Bielefeld, 1898, p. 125) has indeed understood that Lomazzo was describing a sitting Leda, similar to the one by Correggio (now Berlin, No. 218). Michelangelo's *Leda*, finished in 1530 and taken one year later to France, could certainly be described as '*col cigno in grembo*'. Michelangelo's *Leda*, as we know from Vasari, was also in Fontainebleau. My suspicion is that Lomazzo confused the two pictures. (Cf. Goldscheider, *Michelangelo Drawings*, London, 1951, plate 173, and p. 42.) There is an old unwarrantable story that Leonardo's *Leda* was burnt in about 1700 at the instigation of Madame de Maintenon, when she had become old and pious, and Queen of France, and was indeed not in favour of lascivious paintings. According to another report Michelangelo's *Leda* was already burnt, in about 1640, under Louis XIII, by his minister Desnoyers.

16. It is uncertain whether this is the same picture, or only a copy, because the original might have been burned, together with Michelangelo's *Leda*, in about 1640. (See footnote 15.)

It remains doubtful, whether the painting of a *Standing Leda* at Fontainebleau was an original work of Leonardo, or a painted copy from his cartoon, perhaps by Melzi. All the versions which have come down to us are only free copies, most of them by Milanese painters, none of them from Leonardo's workshop, some even by Netherlanders who worked in Italy.[17]

38

DRAPERY STUDY FOR A KNEELING WOMAN. Windsor, 12521
Seidlitz and Popham connected the drawing with Verrocchio's Baptism of Christ (plate 43), Venturi with the Annunciation (plate 59), Sir Kenneth Clark with the Madonna of the Rocks in the National Gallery. I cannot see that Leonardo used this drapery study in any of his paintings; it was probably done for an Adoration of the Child (compare plate 70).

39

DRAPERY STUDY FOR A KNEELING WOMAN. Rome, Galleria Corsini. No. 125770.
Drawing of a figure with folded hands, either for an Adoration of the Child, or else for an Annunciation. Popp connected this drawing with the *Louvre Annunciation* (plate I-c) pointing out that it was not used for the Madonna but for the angel, in a reversed way, as seen in a mirror. Baldass connected it with the drapery of the angel in plate 59, where it also would have been used in a reversed way.

40 and 41

DRAPERY STUDIES FOR THE MADONNA IN THE ST ANNE PAINTING. Windsor, 12532 and 12530. (Compare plate 68.) Both drawings are done with the brush in lamp black and white over black chalk; No. 40 is on red paper, and the hand in red chalk; No. 41, the drapery for a seated figure is on yellowish paper.

42

DRAPERY STUDY FOR THE RIGHT ARM OF ST PETER. Windsor, 12546. For *The Last Supper* (plate 73). Compare also with 57, 63, and 69.

17. For a list of those copies see Seidlitz, p. 528; and Sirén, p. 187 f., with some illustrations. The best copy is the one reproduced here; others are in the possession of the Duke of Pembroke, Wilton House, in the Borghese Gallery, Rome; in the Collection of Mr. David Edge, London (formerly Doetsch and Richeton Collections; the twist of Leda's body in this copy is very similar to that in Raphael's pen and ink sketch). The copy in the Johnson Collection, Philadelphia, is Netherlandish. For original Leonardo drawings of the *Head of Leda* see plates 10 and 11.

Zoan Andrea: The dancing muses, detail of an engraving after Mantegna's *Parnassus*, about 1497. (B. XIII, 305).

Domenico Ghirlandaio: Dancing Maidens, pen and ink drawing, about 1490. Stockholm, National Museum.

43

KNEELING ANGEL IN PROFILE. Detail from Verrocchio's *Baptism of Christ* (Florence, Uffizi), reproduced here in about one third of the original size.

Painted for the Church of the Monastery of San Salvi fuori la Porta alla Croce, at Florence. The inception of the picture by Verrocchio seems to date from about 1470 (according to Planiscig and Sandberg-Vavalà) or else from 1472 (Heydenreich). In its present state it is unfinished in parts, uneven in quality, and a work of several brushes or at least of several periods. Leonardo's share in this painting was first mentioned in 1510, by Francesco Albertini ('*uno angelo di Leonardo Vinci*'), and discussed, forty years later, by Vasari. In more recent times Bayersdorfer and Bode have tried to define Leonardo's contribution to the painting. The wooded cliffs on the right, and the lifeless palm on the left are obviously not by the same hand as the landscape above the two angels (plate 73) which is neither a decorative background nor a conventional rendering of stone, vegetation and water, but the portrait of an individual piece of nature.

Leonardo's share in this painting are the angel in profile on the left, the tuft of grass underneath him, and the landscape above him; nothing else. The head of the angel is damaged and much restored. The finest bit of what Leonardo added to Verrocchio's painting is the drapery of this angel.

If we compare Leonardo's first dated drawing of 1473 (plate 81) with the 'Baptism' landscape (plate 73), there remains little doubt that they both belong to the same period.

44

ST JOHN THE BAPTIST. Windsor, 12572

According to Valentiner, a sketch for a figure in the Pistoia altar-piece. See our note on plate I of the appendix and the illustration on p. 27. In 1478 Leonardo was in Pistoia; this drawing is of the same time, but it might have been done for the San Bernardino Altar-piece, which certainly included a figure of St John. (See footnote 18 on p. 31.) Antonio Billi and the Anonimo Gaddiano mention an early *St John* by Leonardo.

45

DANCING MAIDENS. Venice, 233

The draperies of the maidens remind one of the angels in Botticelli's *Nativity*, dated 1500 (National Gallery, London), but still more of the dancing muses in Mantegna's *Parnassus*, about 1497 (Louvre, No. 1375), once in the studio of Isabella d'Este at Mantua. Was Leonardo influenced by Mantegna, or were he and the other painters inspired by a Hellenistic relief of the Horae? Of course, similar drawings, though not of the same quality, were produced in the workshops of Ghirlandaio and other Florentine artists.

The figure on the left in No. 45 is, curiously enough, dressed like a Fortuna (cf. the engraving by Nicoletto da Modena, or the much later painting by Rubens in the Prado). The characteristic part is the piece of garment, held over the head and used as a sail.

46

NEPTUNE. Windsor, 12570. 25.1 × 39.2 cm.

A study for the cartoon, which, according to Vasari, Leonardo did for his 'good friend Antonio Segni'. The

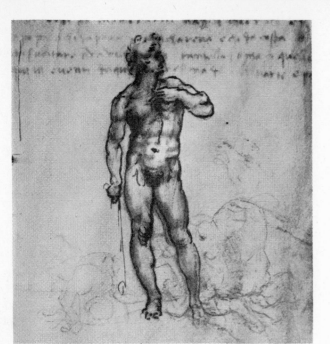

David. Detail of a pen and ink drawing, over black chalk, by Leonardo, c. 1504, after Michelangelo's marble statue. Windsor (12591 r).

47

ALLEGORY OF FORTUNA. British Museum, 1895–9–15–482 (Catal. 1950, No. 104).

This is, I think, Leonardo's most beautiful allegorical drawing, but I do not understand what is meant by it. On the stump of a tree lies a shield, and against the trunk leans a coat-of-arms with a lion rampant. (For a similar escutcheon with lion and dragon, symbolizing strength and prudence, see Richter § 692.) But what do the curves under the shield represent? They can hardly be fluttering ribbons, and are usually explained as flames. Above the shield, touching it with just the toes of one foot, hovers a winged figure, probably meaning Fama. This figure is beautifully shaded in a rather baroque way, and the movement is strongly expressed by the streaming waves of hair and drapery. There is another figure, running towards the tree, holding her garment with one hand and touching the shield with the other hand. This figure is Fortuna, recognizable by her forelock. A part of the same figure, the head turned differently and the hair more elaborately drawn, is repeated in the upper right-hand corner.

According to Popham, 'there seems to be no reason for connecting the angel, or Victory, with the allegorical composition underneath'. Seidlitz and Bodmer, however, take it for *one* consistent composition (and date it to the earliest Milanese years, soon after 1483).

If Leonardo passed through Mantua on his way to Milan in the autumn of 1481, he might have seen a chimney-piece painting of *Fortuna* in the house of Marchese

Allegory of Fortuna ('Occasio'). Painting, probably after a design by Mantegna, c. 1475. Milan.

definite drawing contained many more figures, as Vasari mentions 'sprites, dolphins and winds, and several most beautiful heads of sea gods'.

The motif was perhaps taken from the antique, as were certainly a bronze plaquette in the Dreyfus Collection (Molinier, No. 13), and a plaquette at Dijon (reproduced in *Art Studies*, 1930, fig. 19). The horse at the right, throwing his head sharply sideways, is exactly repeated in Leone Leoni's Andrea Doria Plaquette (Victoria and Albert Museum, No. A484–1910); but a very similar sea-horse is already in an engraving by Mantegna, 'The Combat of Tritons' (B.17), datable c. 1494, and this composition might have inspired Leonardo.

At the top left of the drawing is a note in Leonardo's handwriting: *a bassa i chavalli* (to lower the horses). This, according to Popp and Kenneth Clark, was tried out by Leonardo in the Windsor drawing, No. 12591, of which a part is reproduced here. It is a free copy of Michelangelo's *David*, with a slight sketch of sea-horses under his feet. Only the figure of David is inked-in.[18]

18. In his *Life of Michelangelo* Vasari hints that the younger artist received his commission for the *David* in competition with Leonardo: 'Some of Michelangelo's friends wrote from Florence urging him to return, as they did not want that block of marble in the *opera* [the office of works for the Cathedral] to be spoiled which Piero Soderini, then *gonfaloniere* for life in Florence, had repeatedly proposed to give to Leonardo da Vinci.' Edmondo Solmi (*Rassegna d'Arte*, 1912, p. 128 f.) argued that the Windsor drawing No. 12591 was an independent sketch by Leonardo (not a copy after Michelangelo's *David*, or a development of Windsor drawing No. 12570). It is indeed difficult to imagine how David, as he appears in Leonardo's sketch, could have been transformed into a Neptune, without at least changing the position of both arms.

Biondo (now in the Palazzo Ducale). The similarity consists, however, only in the subject and in the arrangement of the two main figures.

48

STUDY FOR THE ADORATION OF THE KINGS. Louvre (Gallichon Collection), R.F.1978 (cf. plate 49).

In March 1481 Leonardo made a contract with the monks of San Donato a Scopeto, a cloister outside Florence near the Porta Romana, to paint for them an altar-piece and to finish it in two years, or at most in two and a half years. The theme was 'The Adoration of the Kings'. The picture was never finished.[19]

A number of beautiful drawings are connected with this commission (see plates 32 and 58 and 102; but there are many more). No. 48 represents Leonardo's first idea for the painting. The scene is the courtyard of a ruined palace; at the left are two arcades, at the right five arcades and two flights of stairs, leading to a gallery, on which a man is sitting and blowing a trumpet. In the background are many figures, among them men on horseback, somewhat similar to the later sketches for the Anghiari battle. Most of the figures are drawn in the nude, in order to delineate the movements in a manner anatomically correct. The arms of the man who gives the goblet to the child are sketched in two different positions.

For a separate detailed drawing for the background see plate 58.

49–53

THE ADORATION OF THE KINGS. Uffizi, No. 1594. Wood, 258×243 cm.

The picture is just 'under-painted', a large drawing in umber brown over a sand-coloured priming. The most important figures – the Virgin and the Kings in the foreground – are the least-finished ones. The picture was begun in March 1481; when Leonardo left for Milan (probably in the autumn of 1482) the painting remained with Amerigo de' Benci, the father of Ginevra (see plate 23). Professor Simon Meller expressed the opinion that Leonardo resumed his work during his later stay in Florence, i.e. 1503, when he was working on the cartoon of the Anghiari battle; Strzygowski accepted this view, and thought that some of the horses

were added later. Although the whole picture looks as if it were done at one stroke, some of the drawings would seem to confirm this theory. This theory, of course, rests on slender foundations, but I mention it as being worthy of reconsideration.[20]

To understand how it was that Leonardo worked for so considerable a time at his 'Adoration of the Kings' and still left it 'unfinished', we may compare any one of Rembrandt's etchings, which, though of a different period and style, are nearest in artistic aim to Leonardo's Adoration. Let us take one of the best known, the Three Crosses (B. 78). Here, as in Leonardo's Adoration, stand some of the most important figures as white patches against the dark background or a dark group of figures. There exist several 'states' of this etching, comprising a greater or lesser number of figures and different shadings; here we can follow all the stages of work at which in Leonardo's painting we can only guess. Although Rembrandt must have worked for a very long time at this etching, it does not show the least degree of 'finish', not even as much as an average draughtsman could achieve in a few hours of work. We would not, however, call Rembrandt's Three Crosses unfinished; we can see quite well how the etching remained through all its states; and after all the laborious work done, the first creative idea was still in evidence like a brilliant improvisation. Leonardo's painting is no less finished than Rembrandt's etching.

This suggestion of 'sketchiness', indication instead of definition, last thoughts which look like first thoughts, is not altogether a modern idea. Vasari refers to it, in the Life of Luca della Robbia, whose highly finished Cantoria he compares with that of Donatello which is, as he thinks, but a sketch. 'Experience shows', says Vasari, 'that all works of art seen at a distance, whether paintings or sculptures, are bolder and more vigorous to the eye, if merely done in the rough, than if laboriously finished. . . . It often happens that these rapid sketches, which are thrown off suddenly in the first ardour of inspiration, express the idea perfectly in a few strokes; while too much care and labour, on the contrary, will often deprive the works of all force and character when the artist never knows when to take his hands off. . . . The artist who visualizes from the first what he is going to create, invariably proceeds on his

19. The commission was subsequently given to Filippino Lippi, who finished his Adoration of the Kings in March 1497 (1496, according to the Florentine calendar). The monastery of San Donato was destroyed during the siege of Florence in 1529; Filippino's 'Adoration' is now in the Uffizi, No. 1566.

20. In the Venice Academy there is a drawing by Cesare da Sesto, The Adoration of the Kings, in which the Madonna closely resembles Raphael's Madonna of Foligno; but the horses in the background are obviously taken from the 'Battle of Anghiari'. (Reprod. Morelli, Italian Painters, II, p. 91.)

A Leonardo drawing, acquired in 1953 by the British Museum, St George and the Dragon, is clearly based on the jousting horsemen in the upper right corner of No. 49; one horseman is directly copied, the other is transformed into a dragon (plates 103–104).

Outline copy of Leonardo's 'Uffizi Adoration', published by Müller-Walde, 1898. (This outline copy, omitting the uneven modulation of the original painting, gives a clear idea of the arrangement of the sixty or seventy figures of men and horses in the picture.)

way towards perfect realization with ease. . . . Nevertheless, there are some, though they are rare, who can only do well when they proceed slowly . . . as [among the poets] Bembo who expends months and even years in the production of a sonnet.'

Leonardo was a slow worker, and he never brought the Sforza monument beyond the stage of a model, nor some of his finest pictorial compositions beyond the stage of a 'cartoon'. If we are to credit Vasari, he left the *Last Supper* and the *Mona Lisa* 'unfinished', while we can see for ourselves that the *Ambrosiana Musician*, the *Lady with the Ermine*, and the *Adoration of the Kings* are all unfinished. But it is a moot point whether some works are capable of further elaboration without loss.

Leonardo's almost monochrome painting 'Adoration of the Kings' has a charm which no reproduction can communicate.

See also plates 32, 58 and 103.

54

CARTOON FOR THE VIRGIN AND CHILD WITH ST ANNE AND THE INFANT ST JOHN. London, Royal Academy of Arts (Burlington House), No. 183. 139×101 cm.

There are at least three versions of Leonardo's St Anne composition.

(*a*) The first Milanese version, done shortly before Leonardo left the town, c. 1499 (Cartoon in the Royal Academy, London). See plate 54.[21]

(*b*) The Florentine version, as described by Fra Pietro da Novellara, 1501. (See Documents, No. XI, and plate 18.) This cartoon is lost.

(*c*) The second Milanese version, done during Leonardo's subsequent stay in the town, 1508–10. Painting in the Louvre; cartoon lost. (See plate 68.)

There are, besides, a number of tentative drawings, which in my opinion do not correspond with either of the three versions but suggest independent solutions.

Padre Sebastiano Resta (about 1696) saw the St Anne cartoon (plate 54) in Milan, in the collection of Conte Arconati. The cartoon came into the collection of Marchese Casnedi, where it remained until at least 1722; a few years later it was in the collection of Conte Sagredo at Venice, where it was bought by Robert Udny, the brother of the English Ambassador, in 1763. It became the property of the Royal Academy at a date prior to the 23rd March, 1791.

The witness who saw this cartoon in 1722 in the Casnedi collection at Milan is Edward Wright: 'A Holy Family, the same which is painted in S. Celsus.'[22] Langton Douglas (1944, p. 41) did not hesitate to identify this cartoon with the one now in the Royal Academy, London.

55

ST JOHN THE BAPTIST. Louvre, No. 1597. See Document XVI, p. 39. Panel, 69×57 cm.

Louis XIII of France gave the picture to Charles I, in exchange for a painting by Holbein and one by Titian. In 1649, when the King's collection was sold by auction, Leonardo's St John was bought by the banker Jabach on behalf of Cardinal Mazarin, from whom the picture passed to Louis XIV.

The picture is entirely by Leonardo's own hand, but damaged in parts and retouched.

56

MADONNA WITH THE FRUIT-PLATE. Paris, Louvre, No. 101. 33×25 cm. Cf. plate 57.

21. This cartoon is not identical with the one described by Fra Pietro Novellara in 1501, which was done for an altar-piece in S. Annunziata after Filippino Lippi had resigned the commission in favour of Leonardo. The altar-piece has never been executed by Leonardo and the cartoon is lost.

22. Luini's *Holy Family* (now in the Ambrosiana; Suida, p. 130 and fig. 315) is a picture which is based on Leonardo's *St Anne cartoon*. – The church of S. Celso in Milan has been completely altered, and half of it was pulled down in 1826.

57

59-62

MADONNA BENOIS. Hermitage, Leningrad. No. 2773 (Cat. 1916, No. 1981). Painted on wood, transferred to canvas, 48×31.5 cm.

Since 1914 in the Hermitage, formerly in the Collection of Madame Léon Benois (after whom the picture is named; her grandfather had bought it in Astrakhan, from an Italian, in 1824). One of Leonardo's earliest paintings, and one which was endlessly repeated, not only by Italian painters but also by the Flemish school. The best of these replicas is in the Galleria Colonna at Rome, ascribed to Filippino Lippi or sometimes to Lorenzo di Credi (Photo Alinari 7342). Other copies are in the collection of the Earl Spencer, at Althorp, and in the Magdeburg Museum (with the figure of St Joseph added); another copy, rather in the style of Botticini, was in the Toscanelli sale, Florence 1883 (repr. Reinach, *Répertoire*, I, 109). The Madonna alone was copied by Raphael, in his 'Virgin with the Carnation' (of which the original is lost, but several copies are known; cf. Crowe and Cavalcaselle, I, p. 273). The Child alone was often copied, for instance, by Lorenzo di Credi in a Madonna painting in the Turin Gallery, No. 115 (Photo Alinari 14814).

The numerous repetitions of this little painting prove indeed that it cannot have been by a second-rate painter. The picture is not too well preserved; it suffered when it was transferred from panel to canvas; there are retouchings in the drapery, mouth, neck and hands of the Madonna, left knee and right hand of the child, most of the background, etc. Before restoration, the window probably contained a landscape, as the copy in the Galleria Colonna does.

Bodmer, and others, assumed that this little picture was painted, in about 1478, by young Leonardo 'with the help of pupils'. Thiis ascribed it to Sogliani. Heydenreich calls it 'unfinished'; he believes it to be a workshop production, on which Leonardo worked again after 1500 (cf., for the lower part of the drapery, plate 41). It seems to me that all this criticism is caused only by the poor preservation of this genuine early painting.

A sketch in the British Museum (Cat. No. 100 verso), a Madonna and Child, corresponds with the picture.

See the reproduction in full colour on p. 26.

58

STUDY FOR THE BACKGROUND OF THE ADORATION OF THE KINGS. Uffizi, I, 436.
See the notes on plates 48 and 49.

This is mainly a study of perspective; most of the lines are drawn with a ruler. All the figures are put in pen and ink on top of the linear construction.

THE ANNUNCIATION. Uffizi, No. 1618. Panel, 98×217 cm.

See also plates 86 and 98.

Painted for the Convent of Monte Oliveto near Florence; neither the name of the painter nor the date of the painting are documented.

Since 1867 in the Uffizi.

Maud Cruttwell ascribed the picture to Verrocchio. Morelli considered it to be the work of Ridolfo Ghirlandaio, Berenson thought it a joint work of Credi and Leonardo. Baron Liphart, who was the first to claim the Benois Madonna for Leonardo, was also the first to claim this painting for him. Now almost generally considered to be an early work of Leonardo's.

At the age of twenty, in 1472, Leonardo was made a member of the Guild of St Luke, which means he was allowed to accept independent commissions as a painter. The *Annunciation* might have been the first commission he ever received. At that time, however, and even four years later, he was still working as an assistant in Verrocchio's studio and staying in his house. Perugino became a member of the Guild of St Luke in the same year as Leonardo and he also worked in Verrocchio's workshop. Lorenzo di Credi, who is recorded in the same workshop between 1480 and 1488, probably began there as an apprentice in about 1472. Botticelli became a member of the Guild of St Luke in the same year as Perugino and Leonardo, 1472, and, I believe, was at that time also employed as an assistant in Verrocchio's workshop. There were several other assistants. Whether the commission for the *Annunciation* was given to Leonardo, or to his master Verrocchio, it was probably painted in Verrocchio's house and there one or the other of the assistants might have helped with it; but certainly not Lorenzo di Credi, who at that time was only a boy of fourteen. Heydenreich assumes that the Angel is from the hand of Leonardo, but not the Madonna.

Miss Cruttwell had already detected that the curious ornamentation of the reading-desk (plate 62) bore resemblance to Verrocchio's Medici Sarcophagus. The resemblance to the sarcophagus of Desiderio da Settignano's *Marsuppini monument* (ill. in Galassi's *La Scultura Fiorentina del Quattrocento*, 1949, plate 271), in which Verrocchio is said to have participated, is even stronger.

For the drapery of the Angel see plate 39.

The two parts of the landscape, though painted in an orange evening light (plate 86), are rather in the spirit of Ghirlandaio; but 'the flowering carpet of plants' is highly original, based on direct observation of nature and technically related to much later work of Leonardo's (plate 98).

The picture is somewhat obscured by an old varnish which has turned yellow in parts. The tip of the angel's wing appears to be repainted.

In 1907 Sidney Colvin published the drawing for the right arm of the angel, which drawing is certainly by the young Leonardo.

Leonardo: Study for the right arm of the Angel of the *Annunciation* (plate 59). About 1472. Oxford, Christ Church.

63

MADONNA WITH THE CARNATION.
Munich, Ältere Pinakothek, No. 7779

Panel, 62×47 cm. Cut at the left side, of about 4 cm.

The picture is in a very poor condition, which can be seen even in the reproduction; the face of the Virgin, for instance, is nearly completely overpainted, forming a leathery *craquelure*. But, allowing for the bad preservation of the painting, a long list can be given connecting the Munich Madonna with the workshop of Verrocchio:

(1) Madonna by Credi, Munich 7820.
(2) The Pistoia Altar-piece (Detail, *Madonna*, plate I–b), illustr. p. 169.
(3) Madonna Dreyfus (plate I–a), illustr. p. 169.
(4) An altar-piece by Credi in Naples (Mackowsky, *Verrocchio*, fig. 77).
(5) A silver-point drawing by Verrocchio (sometimes ascribed to Credi) in Dresden (B.B. 672, fig. 139).
(6) A Head of the Madonna in the Louvre, drawing (Suida, fig. 4: attributed to Leonardo).
(7) A Head by Verrocchio in the British Museum (Cat. 1950, No. 258 r.).

Comparing the black chalk drawing in the British Museum with the head of the Madonna in the Munich picture (plate 63), we certainly find the same eyes, mouth and hair-dress, and we can even assume that the same model was used. A comparison with the other paintings mentioned in the list (which could be extended) would give a similar result; the brooch and the long fold underneath are significant.

The Munich picture was certainly executed in Verrocchio's workshop; the landscape, the draperies, and the vase of flowers, all favour an attribution to Leonardo. But still it is an unpleasant picture.

Berenson, Kenneth Clark, and Heydenreich think that Leonardo collaborated in this work to some extent; Baldass thinks Leonardo had probably no share in it; he emphasizes that even the *composition* of the picture cannot be by him;[23] Fabriczy thought the picture was composed by Leonardo but finished by Credi; Hildebrandt had a similar opinion; according to Bode, Suida, Venturi, and Valentiner, it is an early work of Leonardo's; some other writers suggested that it was an early work of Credi's; Bodmer assumed that it was either a replica or a free version of a lost Madonna painting by Leonardo.

The pedigree of the picture does not go back beyond 1889 when it was bought, from a private collection in Bavaria, by Bayersdorfer for the Munich Gallery and exhibited there as a Leonardo.

64

MADONNA OF THE ROCKS. Louvre, No. 1599. Painted on wood (transferred to canvas), 197× 119.5 cm.

On April 25th, 1483, Leonardo and the brothers Evangelista and Ambrogio de Predis received the commission for this altar-piece from the Confraternity of the Immaculate Conception, Milan. This picture was finished in 1485, or perhaps a little later; this is the first version of the *Madonna of the Rocks*, now in the *Louvre*. Adolfo Venturi contended that King Louis XII took this painting to France, which is credible enough, as that King even attempted to have Leonardo's *Last Supper* cut from the wall. If Venturi is right, the *Madonna of the Rocks* had already been in France for some time when Leonardo arrived there; however, we cannot be certain about this, as no mention is made of the picture being in France until 1625, when it was at Château de Fontainebleau.

Heydenreich (1954, p. 435 f.) suggested that the picture might have been taken already by Ludovico Sforza from

23. Ludwig Baldass, in *Zeitschrift für Kunstwissenschaft*, VII, 1953, p. 175, n. 25.

the chapel of the Confraternity. This does not contradict Venturi's theory; Louis XII could have carried the picture away from the Duke's castle.

According to Heydenreich, the second version of the *Madonna of the Rocks* was begun by Leonardo and Ambrogio de Predis in about 1495. Then a lawsuit followed, which lasted for over ten years, as Predis insisted on supplementary payment. In April 1506 the Confraternity agreed to an additional payment. Leonardo came to Milan in May 1506, received 100 lire in 1507, went back to Florence, came again in July 1508, and received again 100 lire. Soon afterwards the *Madonna of the Rocks* was placed in the Chapel of the Confraternity in the Church of San Francesco, where it remained until 1781. It was sold, and in 1785 it was brought to England; at one time it belonged to Lord Suffolk, and in 1880 it was bought by the National Gallery. (About this second version of the altar-piece see also note on plate 65.)

The Louvre version suffered when it was transferred from panel to canvas (which was done about 1800); it has been retouched in many places, especially in the drapery of the Virgin, and the lower part of the background. The varnish has turned yellow and is falsifying the colours. See also plates 78, 90 and 99.

65

MADONNA OF THE ROCKS. National Gallery, London, No. 1093. Painted on wood, 189.5×120 cm. See the note on No. 64; and for the whole very complicated problem, Martin Davies, *The Virgin of the Rocks*, 1947; also the same author's National Gallery Catalogue, London, 1951, 'The Earlier Italian Schools', pp. 204–219. (Against Davies's early dating of the Louvre version, see Valentiner in the Catalogue of the Leonardo exhibition at the Los Angeles County Museum, 1949, p. 61; and against Davies's interpretation of the sources, see Heydenreich, 1954, p. 436, footnote.) Most writers assume that Predis and other assistants had an important share in the painting of this second version; only Bode (*Studien über Leonardo da Vinci*, 1921, p. 82) decided: 'The *Madonna of the Rocks* in London, from the church of S. Francesco in Milan, is doubtless an original by Leonardo, and not a replica painted by Predis; if he took any share in it at all, it can only have been in some unimportant details.' According to Suida, most of the paint was put on by Leonardo (*Leonardo und sein Kreis*, 1929, p. 49 f.); both children, the head of the angel, the hand of the Virgin, the draperies and all the flowers are, according to Suida, painted by the master himself. Kenneth Clark (1958, p. 128 f.) is of a similar opinion, praising particularly the angel's head; but he does not deny that it is a workshop production.

The two wings of the altar-piece (National Gallery, London, Nos. 1661 and 1662) are not by Leonardo. The left wing, an angel in green, was probably executed in the Predis workshop; the right wing, an angel in red, has tentatively been ascribed by Kenneth Clark to Ferrando de Llanos (p. 53 and p. 129).

The central panel of the altar-piece was cleaned in 1949. See also plate 95.

66

STUDY FOR THE HEAD OF THE 'MADONNA LITTA'. Louvre, No. 2376

According to Berenson (*Florentine Drawings*, second edition, No. 1067C, and p. 562), one of the earliest drawings by Leonardo. Seidlitz was of the same opinion. Demonts and Bodmer date it about 1490–94, Kenneth Clark about 1480. For the dating of this drawing compare No. 20, which is related in style.

Seidlitz thought that Ambrogio de Predis strengthened the outlines of the profile when he pressed them through with a stylus on to the panel on which he painted the 'Madonna Litta' (plate 67).

67

MADONNA LITTA. Hermitage, Leningrad, No. 249 (Cat. 1891 and 1916, No. 13a). Painted on wood, transferred to canvas, 42×33 cm.

The picture is named after Conte Litta, Milan, in whose collection it was before it came to the Hermitage, in 1865. The Hermitage Catalogue tries to identify it with a picture which was in 1543 in the Contarini collection at Venice.

The painting is in a bad state of preservation and completely retouched. It is usually ascribed to Boltraffio, or to Ambrogio de Predis. There is no doubt that it is based on drawings by Leonardo (see plate 66).

Morelli attributed it to Bernardino de' Conti, but there is a replica by this painter in the Museo Poldi-Pezzoli in Milan (No. 639), very different in quality from the Hermitage painting. Many other replicas of the Madonna Litta are known.

According to Marie Herzfeld, the *Madonna Litta* is by the same painter as the *Resurrection of Christ with S. Lucia and S. Lionardo* (Berlin Museum, No. 90B). This very uneven picture, of which small parts are remarkably fine, seems to me to be painted by Ambrogio de Predis in about 1508, at a time when he helped Leonardo with the second version of the *Madonna of the Rocks*, and when Leonardo was always about to help him; and did so indeed by designing the two saints in the *Resurrection of Christ*.

68–69

VIRGIN AND CHILD WITH ST ANNE
AND THE INFANT ST JOHN. Louvre, No. 1598.
Wood, 170×129 cm.

See note on plate 54; and plate 79.

Most of this painting was done by pupils; only the
landscape, the figure of St Anne and the right arm of the
Virgin are outstanding. It might be thought that the
assistant was Melzi, but in this case it is inexplicable why
Melzi did not finish the picture, as he took it with him
to Italy, after Leonardo's death.

The picture is not in a good condition. The outlines
have been strengthened by a restorer; a dark, yellow
varnish has obscured the colours. In the detail photograph, plate 69, we have tried, by means of a long
exposure, to penetrate through the yellow varnish. A
few blue patches in the sky show the original colour;
the cloak of the Madonna was originally also of a purer
blue, the flesh less red.

In 1517, Cardinal Luigi d'Aragona saw the *St Anne* in
Leonardo's studio (cf. Document No. XVI, on p. 39).
Paolo Giovio, in about 1527, stated that Francis I owned
Leonardo's *St Anne* painting; but Giovio was never in
France and he probably meant a cartoon. When Melzi
returned to Italy, he took the drawings and pictures,
left to him by Leonardo in his Will, to Italy; amongst
them the *St Anne* painting. When Cardinal Richelieu
crossed into Italy, in 1629, to settle the Mantuan suc-
cession question by war, he found the picture in Casale,
a town on the river Po, bought it, brought it to Paris
and presented it to the King. Since 1801 it has been in
the Louvre.

70

STUDIES FOR THE ADORATION OF THE
CHILD. Metropolitan Museum, New York

Here an idea is developed which first appeared in the
sketches for 'The Adoration of the Shepherds'. The
drawing is still closer to the 'Adoration' than to the
'Madonna of the Rocks'.

A passage in the Vasari biography refers to a *natività*
painting by Leonardo: 'Ludovico Sforza begged
Leonardo to paint an altar-piece of the Nativity, which
was sent by the Duke to the Emperor'.[24] As this paint-

24. According to Vasari, this painting, now lost, was done soon
after Leonardo's arrival in Milan. The Anonimo Gaddiano (ed. Frey,
p. 112) mentions the picture as being in the possession of Maximilian I, and Carducho (*Dialogos*, p. 20) as in the Collection of
Charles V. (Professor H. Siebenhüner, in a footnote to his Vasari
edition, 1940, p. 297, suggests that this *Nativity* was nothing but the
Louvre version of the *Madonna of the Rocks*. This is an ingenious,
though not easily acceptable idea.)

Adoration of the Child. Silver-point drawing by Leonardo.
Windsor, No. 12560 (detail).

Kneeling Madonna. Pen and ink drawing by Leonardo,
Milan, Ambrosiana (Cod. Atl. 358 r., detail).

ing is lost we cannot with any certainty connect the
drawing with it.

A small sketch at Windsor (No. 12560), and another,
very slight one, in the Codice Atlantico are for the same
composition as plate 87. Several versions of a painting,
The Madonna with the playing children, can be connected
with these drawings. (Bodmer 78, 79; another version
in the Budapest Museum; and the best one in the
Ashmolean Museum, Oxford, from the collection of
Henry Harris.) All those paintings are probably based
on a (lost) cartoon by Leonardo.

PLATE I. *Paintings by Lorenzo di Credi.* (a) *The Dreyfus Madonna* (attributed to Leonardo by Suida, Langton Douglas, Degenhart, a.o.) Washington, Kress Collection. – (b) *Madonna and Child.* Detail from the Altar-piece in Pistoia Cathedral, painted 1475-85. – (c) *Annunciation.* Detail from a predella panel of the Pistoia Altar-piece (painted with the help of Leonardo?). Paris, Louvre. – (d) *San Donato and the Tax Collector.* Part of the same predella (attributed to Leonardo by Bayersdorfer, Valentiner, Suida, and Langton Douglas). Worcester, U.S.A., Art Museum.

PLATE II. Leonardo: *Portraits of Duke Ludovico Sforza and Duchess Beatrice, with their children*, 1497. (Details from Montorfano's *Crucifixion*.) Milan, S. Maria delle Grazie.

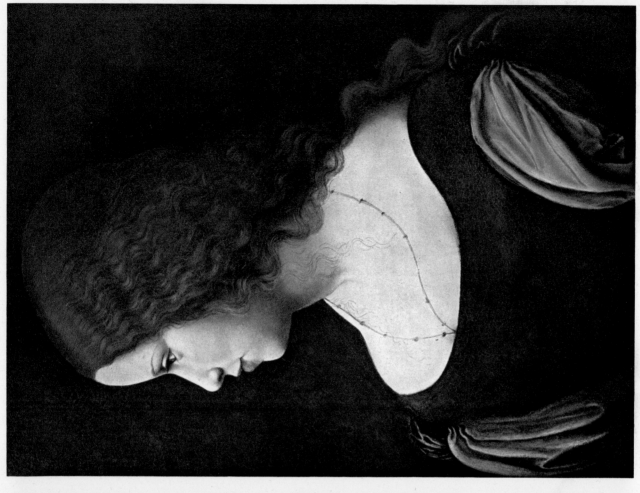

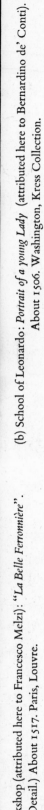

(b) School of Leonardo: *Portrait of a young Lady* (attributed here to Bernardino de' Conti).
About 1506. Washington, Kress Collection.

PLATE III. (a) Leonardo Workshop (attributed here to Francesco Melzi): *"La Belle Ferronnière"*.
(Detail.) About 1517. Paris, Louvre.

PLATE IV. (a) Leonardo: *Rough Sketch for the 'Last Supper'*. About 1495. Windsor Castle (No. 12542).
(b) Leonardo: *The Last Supper*. Engraving by Raffaello Morghen after a drawing by Teodoro Matteini (published in 1800).

71–72

SKETCH FOR THE LAST SUPPER. Venice, 254. 26×39 cm.

This is a very important drawing as far as the composition is concerned. In my opinion, it is a copy, by a pupil, after Leonardo's first cartoon (or large drawing) for the *Last Supper*; the names of the Apostles are added in Leonardo's handwriting. No. 72 shows how the cartoon must have looked originally: the sheet used by the copyist for the Venice Academy drawing was too short to take all the figures, the four Apostles who should be at the left are placed underneath, but the shoulder and arm of one of them are given twice, with all the accidental features of the sketch exactly repeated. Otherwise the copy is rather weak, the hands especially being awkwardly drawn; but the copyist followed the original very closely as he even imitated the shading from left to right. (Cf. Beltrami, in *Boll. della Racc. Vinc.* 1910.) Berenson and Bodmer accept this drawing as genuine; and so does Popham (p. 118) who thinks that Leonardo himself copied here one of his earlier drawings. Kenneth Clark (1958, p. 94) accepts it too, although apparently with some doubts. Another sketch for the *Last Supper* (plate IV–a), which must date from the same time, is very different in character. Giglioli (*Leonardo*, 1944, p. 116) thinks that the drawing is by Leonardo, but of the handwriting only three words.

In these first sketches Leonardo followed the Florentine tradition in placing Judas isolated on one side of the table and figuring St John sleeping with his head on his arms; we find the same arrangement of figures in Castagno's 'Cenacolo' at Florence; or also in Ghirlandaio's; or Francesco Botticini's at Empoli.

73–75

THE LAST SUPPER. Santa Maria delle Grazie, Milan. Wall-painting, 420×910 cm.

See Documents, Nos. VII and VIII.

Painted at the instance of Duke Ludovico Moro for the dining-room of the Cloister of the Dominican monks of Santa Maria delle Grazie. The building is no longer used as a monastery, but Leonardo's painting is still there, or at least the ruins of it. A door, leading to the kitchen, was cut through the middle of the lower part of the painting. Already Leonardo's contemporaries were complaining about the poor state of preservation of the Last Supper. What we can see of it at the present time is the original grand composition which could not be obliterated, patches of the old paint here and there, and the work of generations of restorers. The first restoration took place in 1726, the next in 1770; during the French occupation, 1796–1815, the painting was exposed to

much damage; in 1800 the Refectory was used as a forage-room by the soldiers; afterwards, between 1820 and 1908, it was thoroughly restored three times.[25] And yet this greatest of paintings, prior to Michelangelo's and Raphael's Vatican Frescoes, still radiates vitality, just as a tragedy of Sophocles speaks to us again even in the poorest translation, or the Parthenon frieze through mutilated and broken fragments.

Some beautiful drawings were left finished by Leonardo in preparation for his wall-painting – see Nos. 9, 14–17. The three lunettes above the *Last Supper*, with the Sforza coat-of-arms surrounded by garlands of fruit, are also from the hand of Leonardo; they had been whitewashed, probably in the 18th century, and were uncovered in 1854, when the whole painting was restored (mainly by fixing the flaking paint with wax to the wall). There is very little left now of those lunette paintings (plates 73 and 89).

76–77

ST JEROME. Pinacoteca Vaticana, No. 337 (151). Panel, 103×75 cm.

The authenticity of this painting has never been doubted, though there is no literary documentation to it and it is not mentioned in any of the old Leonardo biographies. Poggi and Rinaldis assume that it was painted immediately before Leonardo left for Milan,[26] i.e. about 1481–82. (Cf. the head at the right of plate 52, which is of the same period.)

The painting was found by Cardinal Fesch (c. 1820) in a second-hand shop in Rome; it was being used as the door of a small wardrobe, the head of the Saint being cut out. The Cardinal, an uncle of Napoleon, was lucky enough to find the missing part of the panel a few years later – in the workshop of a cobbler, who was using the board as a table-top. In 1845, six years after the Cardinal's death, Pius IX bought the restored painting for his Gallery.

25. The reproductions in the present volume are based on photographs taken after the restoration in 1955 (carried out by Commendatore Mauro Pelliccioli, Milan). Raffaello Morghen's engraving, made before the *Last Supper* had suffered its worst damages, has now almost documentary value, though it contains some minor inaccuracies (plate IV–b).

26. Was this picture done in competition with Perugino? Vasari states that Perugino, while he studied in Florence under Verrocchio, painted a *St Jerome in Penitence* on a wall in the cloister of Camaldoli, and that this mural was 'much valued by the Florentines and greatly praised because he had made the saint old, lean and shrivelled, and wasted to a skeleton.' Leonardo's *St Jerome* belongs to his early Milanese period; for the landscape compare plate 64, for the single figure in a large space compare plate 70, and the illustrations on p. 168. (Perugino is mentioned by Leonardo in the *Codex Atlanticus*: 'A naked figure by Perugino.')

78

CAVE. Detail from the *Madonna of the Rocks*, Louvre, plate 64.

79

A LANDSCAPE OF NAKED MOUNTAINS. Detail from the *St Anne*, Louvre, plate 68.

80

A RAVINE WITH WATER BIRDS. Windsor, 12395

This drawing does not make the same impression of spontaneity as the earlier No. 81, and at least parts of it seem to be drawn from memory. Compare also the monumental landscape from *St Jerome*, which is about three years later (plate 77).

81

ARNO LANDSCAPE. Florence, Uffizi, No. 8P.

Dated by the inscription '*dì di santa Maria della neve addi 5 daghossto 1473*' (the day of the Holy Virgin of the Snows, August the 5th, 1473). According to Seidlitz, this day was celebrated by the Church as the 'day of temptation'; according to Ravaisson-Mollien, the 5th of August was still celebrated in some way by the end of the 19th century on the Rigi in Switzerland as 'the day of Maria in the Snow'.

The writing on the *recto* is from right to left. The *verso* contains a sketch in black chalk, gone over with pen, of a mountainous landscape, with a bridge, the pen-and-ink sketch of a naked running man, and a head; also the note, 'Io morando danto sono chontento'. This is written in the normal way, from left to right, not reversed.

82

HURRICANE (also called 'Apocalyptic Storm' or 'The Deluge'). Windsor, 12376. 27×40.8 cm.

Earlier than the ten drawings of the 'Deluge series', Windsor Nos. 12377-86, of which one is reproduced here as No. 85.

This drawing shows: horsemen thrown to the ground by a hurricane, and an uprooted tree in the lower right corner. In the distance are seen the whirling waves of the sea, clouds, and Storm Gods blowing through pipes or trumpets. The group of six Wind Gods at the left recalls the trumpet-blowing angels in Michelangelo's 'Last Judgement', painted twenty years later.

Popp calls this drawing *Diluvio*, with reference to fol. 6 *verso* in Manuscript G. (Richter, §§ 607-609) and Windsor No. 12665: '. . . inundated valleys, in the depths of which were seen the bending tree-tops . . . Let Aeolus with the Winds be shown entangling the trees floating uprooted, and whirling in the huge waves . . .'

83

STORM IN THE ALPS. Windsor, 12409

I am dating this 'about 1500' in concordance with Popp, Popham and Clark, who are dating it 1499-1500. But it might be a little later. I imagine that these bird's-eye view landscapes were drawn at the time when Leonardo was most interested in the problems of aviation. There is a note in the Leicester Manuscript (Richter § 1060), datable c. 1504-1505, about the weather in the Alps, which reads like a text to this illustration.

84

A BIRD'S-EYE VIEW OF A RIVER LAND-SCAPE, WITH A FERRY BOAT. Windsor, 12400

This drawing is probably not much earlier than the Codex 'About the Flight of Birds', 1505, at the Royal Library, Turin. Similar sketches, e.g., in Manuscript K, are somewhat later.

85

THE DELUGE. Windsor, 12379

The first of the ten drawings at Windsor Castle, which form a series; certainly of a late period, when Leonardo studied intensively the movement of water.

These drawings, despite their almost abstract pattern, convey the reality of a vision.

One of the drawings forming the Deluge series (No. 12381), is only preserved in a copy from a pupil's hand (possibly by Melzi, according to Kenneth Clark).

86

LANDSCAPE. Detail from the *Uffizi Annunciation*. See note on plate 59.

87

LANDSCAPE. Detail from the *Baptism of Christ*. See note on plate 43.

88

PLANT ORNAMENT. Panel, 42×37 cm.

On the reverse of the 'Ginevra de' Benci' portrait. Cut at the lower end by about 20 cm. See note on plate 23.

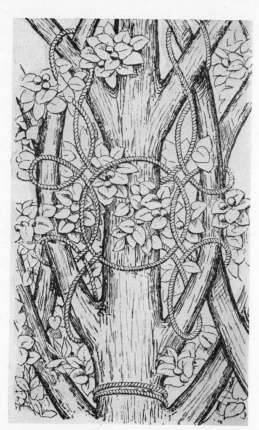

A detail of the original decoration by Leonardo in the Sala delle Asse in the Castello Sforzesco. Copied by Luca Beltrami (*Leonardo da Vinci e la Sala delle Asse*, Milan, 1902).

The central design of this decoration was developed into the abstract ornament of the 'Knots' (see the illustration on p. 12.)

Reconstruction of the painting on the back of the Ginevra panel before cutting. (After Dr. Jens Thiis, 1909.)
Compare plate 88.

89

FRUIT GARLANDS. Detail from a lunette over the *Last Supper*. See note on plate 73.

90

PLANTS. From the Louvre version of the *Madonna of the Rocks* (plate 64)

Plant life in the shadow of the woods is depicted here in a deep *sfumato*. The brush, loaded with a yellowish pigment, went rapidly over the dark ground, producing a kind of clair-obscure (which points forward to the technique Rembrandt sometimes used in painting backgrounds and garments). But Leonardo knew the individual shapes of the plants by heart, and his brush-strokes, in all their speed, reproduced them conscientiously.

91

FLOWERING PLANTS. Windsor, 12424. 19.8× 16 cm.

The large flower is a Star of Bethlehem; the others are a Wood anemone, a stalk of Crowsfoot, etc.

Leonardo was interested in all the organic forms which life is taking, and he drew plants in the same way as portraits, animals, or anatomical details. In a little notebook which he used (between 1490 and 1493) he put down 'Maestro da Marliano has a fine herbal. He lives opposite Strami the carpenters'. Leonardo invented also a method of 'natural impression', which consists in covering a dried leaf or plant with a thin layer of oil paint and printing it off on paper, either white on black or black on white. Leonardo's botanical drawings were probably all done as scientific illustrations; but he used these studies in his cartoons and paintings whenever there was need for them. Even in his earliest works there is some botanical detail which is very well observed and reproduced, e.g. the tuft of grass underneath the Angel he added to Verrocchio's picture (plate 43), or the carpet of flowers in the Uffizi Annunciation (plate 98). He put plants into his (lost) Adam and Eve cartoon, his Madonna with a Vase of Flowers, his Madonna of the Rocks, into the three lunettes above the 'Last Supper', the Leda cartoons and paintings, into the designs he gave to his pupils Melzi and Gianpetrino for their *Colombine*, *Flora*, and *Pomona*. For all those compositions Leonardo used, I should think, studies of plants which he had drawn at *various* dates. The 'wall decoration in the shape of interlaced branches' which Leonardo painted in 1498 on the ceiling of the Sala delle Asse in the Castello Sforzesco at Milan, must once have been very beautiful; what we can see there now is too much restored to be called Leonardo's work; it only shows his invention – a geometrical pattern of plant life formed in a naturalistic way. The restoration of this ceiling painting was prepared by Luca Beltrami in 1884, and he also copied carefully in pen and ink whatever traces he could find of the original work. Those copies he published in 1902, a year after the Milanese painter Ernesto Rusca had ruined Leonardo's work by complete overpainting.

92

ANEMONES. Windsor, 12423

93

STUDIES OF FLOWERS. Venice, Academy, 237

94

LILY. Windsor, 12418. 31.4×17.7 cm.
The earliest of Leonardo's botanical studies, done in a style different from the later drawings; the technique resembles that of the early drapery studies.
I thought for some time it might have been a preparatory study for an altar-piece for San Francesco in Brescia; Leonardo received the commission for it in 1497, but never executed the painting. There is a note in Manuscript I–2, 107a (Richter, § 679), 'Anthony, a lily and a book'. 1497, though, seems too late as a date for Leonardo's drawing, which is of the same period as the *St John*, plate 44. It is probable that Leonardo also designed a 'Madonna of the Lily', of which only copies are extant, one of them at Highnam Court in Gloucester. (Cf. Suida, p. 52.)

95

UNDERGROWTH. Detail from the London version of the *Madonna of the Rocks* (plate 65)

96

FLOWERING RUSHES. Windsor, 12430 *recto*
According to Kenneth Clark, 'done in connection with the *Kneeling Leda*' (cf. plate 36, and illustration on p. 159). The front of the sheet has a pink preparation; the back is white and contains a study of a bulrush with one seed-vessel.

97

OAK-LEAVES WITH ACORNS, etc. Windsor, 12422
Done, according to Malaguzzi Valeri, in connection with the painting of the garlands above the *Last Supper*; but, in their present state, those garlands contain nothing very similar; Bodmer points to the decorations in the Sala della Asse, without believing that the present drawing was actually done for it. Whereas Leonardo's other studies of plants are as flat as they appear in far-eastern painting, this branch of oak-leaves makes a pronounced sculpturesque impression.
Compare the wreath of oak-leaves in plate 2.

98

FLOWERING MEADOW. Detail from the *Uffizi Annunciation*. See note on plate 59.

99

IRISES AND WOOD ANEMONES. Detail from the Louvre version of the *Madonna of the Rocks* (plate 64)

100

A DOG. Windsor, 12361
This drawing is shaded from left to right, and it is certainly genuine. Accepted as an original drawing of Leonardo's by Adolfo Venturi (Comm. Vinc. 130) and Popham (No. 82). Kenneth Clark regarded it as a copy and ascribed it tentatively to Melzi.

101

STUDY OF A BEAR, New York, Lehman Collection.
The bear, and the study of a paw, are drawn in silverpoint over the sketch of a Madonna. This drawing, according to its technique, must be early; it is in fact of the same date as the two similar drawings, the study of *Ox and Ass* at Windsor (plate 102), and the study of *Crabs* in the Cologne Museum.

102

ASS AND OX. Windsor, 12362
Probably a sketch for animals in an *Adoration of the Shepherds*, or *Adoration of the Kings*.

103

FIGHTING HORSEMEN. Detail from the background of the *Adoration of the Kings* (plate 49)
This motive was developed into a *Dragon-Fight* (plate 104); and, twenty years later, to the central group in the *Battle of Anghiari* (plate 108).

104

DRAGON-FIGHT. London, British Museum (1952–10–11–2). Pen and brown ink, with brown wash, over a sketch drawn with the stylus. 13.9×19 cm.
From the collection of George Henry Haydon, who died in 1891; the drawing formed part of a small album belonging to his grand-daughter, Mrs. Winifred Reavell.

105

STUDIES OF A DRAGON-FIGHT. Windsor, 12331. 29.8×21.2 cm.
Other studies for horsemen fighting a dragon are at the Louvre (bequest of Baron Edmond de Rothschild; reprod. Richter I, plate XXXIIIA) and in the Ashmolean Museum, Oxford (reprod. by Colvin); a studio copy of a small drawing at the Ambrosiana, Milan (reprod. Rosenberg, fig. 33; Photo Braun, No. 75043), and the original drawing, now in the British Museum. A note of 1492 by Leonardo, how to draw an imaginary animal (a dragon) so that it should appear natural, is transliterated in Richter, § 585.

The date of this drawing is controversial; it has been dated by various scholars between 1480 and 1514. Bodmer connects it rightly with sketches for the *Battle of Anghiari*, dating the drawing 1505–08 (cf. e.g. BB. 1098).
This drawing, and No. 104, were probably intended for a painting of St George. One of the earliest pictures Raphael painted during his stay in Florence was a St George (which, in 1506, was brought to the King of England by Baldassare Castiglione; now in the Hermitage, Leningrad). It seems probable that Leonardo saw Raphael's composition and felt incited to compose his own, much wilder version.

106

STUDY FOR THE SFORZA MONUMENT. Windsor, 12358 *recto*.
See Document I, on p. 33. In this letter, datable 1482, to Ludovico Sforza of Milan, Leonardo says: 'Again, the bronze horse could be taken up.' From 1479 onward – in the same year Verrocchio received his commission for the Colleoni monument – Ludovico Sforza had

Antonio Pollaiuolo: Drawing for the Sforza monument, about 1480–82.
Munich, Print room.

School of Leonardo: Engraving after small-scale models for the Sforza monument. London, British Museum.

Medicean Gem. Etching in Leonardo Agostini's *Le Gemme Antiche Figurate*, vol.II, 1669.

carried on negotiations in order to find the right artist who could design and cast in bronze a large equestrian monument for Francesco Sforza, his father. In the 'Life of Antonio Pollaiuolo', Vasari says: 'After his death a drawing and a model were discovered for an equestrian monument of Francesco Sforza, Duke of Milan, which he made for Ludovico Sforza'.

Of Pollaiuolo's design two copies are extant, one in the Munich Print room, and one in the Lehman collection, New York.

Pollaiuolo's sketches for an equestrian monument were, according to Kenneth Clark, perhaps imitated by Leonardo; unless both artists based their designs on 'some classical relief'.

The *motif* of the galloping rider trampling down an enemy is known from Roman coins – e.g. one of Lucius Verus, and from antique gems – e.g. Furtwängler, XXV, 52. But a cameo, once in the Medici Collection, shows the foe defending himself with his shield in a very similar position to that in some of Leonardo's drawings, especially when he reverted to the same idea for the Trivulzio monument (see plate 111).

No. 106 belongs to Leonardo's latest and finest silverpoint drawings; he did not use that technique after 1490. The arms of the rider are tentatively sketched in different directions: the left arm, holding the reins, once near the mane, and once drawn back; the right arm with the baton once stretched forward and once backward. The prostrate foe holds a shield over his head. See also footnote 28 on p. 18; also p. 34, and plate VIII. A drawing at Windsor (12357), and an engraving at the British Museum (reproduced here) contain traces of small-scale models for the Sforza monument.

107

STUDIES OF HORSES' LEGS. Turin, Royal Library, No. 15580

108

THE FIGHT FOR THE STANDARD. Copy of the central part of Leonardo's cartoon, *The Battle of Anghiari*. Drawing by Rubens; black chalk, pen and brush; 43.5×56.5 cm. The Hague, Her Royal Highness, Princess Wilhelmina of Holland.

See footnotes 43–46 on pp. 20–21.

A large wall in the Sala del Gran Consiglio of the Palazzo Vecchio in Florence, was to be decorated with two patriotic paintings. In October 1503 Leonardo received a commission for one of those paintings. The section to cover measured about 24 by 60 feet. Leonardo chose as his theme an incident from the war between the Florentines and the Milanese. About ten months

Michelangelo: Copy of a part of Leonardo's *Battle of Anghiari* cartoon. Pen and ink drawing, c. 1504. British Museum.

later Michelangelo was given a commission for the other painting. The section on the wall he agreed to paint had the same measurements as that of Leonardo's painting. He chose a scene from the war against Pisa, the *Battle of Cascina*.

Leonardo finished his cartoon by the end of 1505 and began to paint the centre group on the wall. He never finished his work; on May 30th, 1506, he returned on short leave to Milan; but after that he did not take up this work again.

No complete copy of the lost Anghiari cartoon is preserved – only a few original sketches, many more studies of horses, and a much retouched Head of a Warrior at Oxford (probably only a copy, but apparently in the original size of the cartoon, namely larger than life). There are many copies of the centre scene, the *Fight for the Standard*, including one drawing in the Louvre, attributed to Rubens. Michelangelo and Raphael copied some other parts of Leonardo's cartoon, as has been repeatedly pointed out.

Raphael: Copy of a part of Leonardo's *Battle of Anghiari* cartoon. Silver-point, c. 1505. Oxford, Ashmolean Museum.

According to Cellini, Leonardo's cartoon was in his time still to be seen in the Sala di Papa of the Monastery S. Maria Novella. But according to the Anonimo Gaddiano (see p. 30) Leonardo had taken parts of the

The Fight for the Standard. Engraving from J. B. Séroux d'Agincourt's *Histoire de l'Art par les monuments* (Paris, 1811-23, plate 173-3).

The Calvacade. Black chalk drawing by Leonardo. Windsor, 12339 r. (According to Geymüller, 1886, for the group at the extreme right of the cartoon.)

cartoon with him to France. (Goethe, too, assumed that the cartoon was lost in France.) The original cartoon was of an enormous size (c. 8×20 m.), and had to be left behind in Florence. But Leonardo had certainly made also a *modello* in a smaller size; and perhaps full-size copies in outline (at least of the part he transferred to the wall) in order that there should be no need to cut up the original. We do not know what exactly Leonardo took to France; but those parts of the cartoon may still have existed in France when Rubens arrived there. (Leonardo's wall-painting in Florence did not exist any longer in Rubens's time.)

There is no agreement amongst scholars about the reconstruction of the cartoon. It is, however, now generally agreed that the composition consisted of three parts. Some students believe that if one puts next to the sketches of Michelangelo and Raphael, towards the right, Leonardo's drawing, Windsor, No. 12339 *recto*, (see illustration), it completes the composition. Other students suggested: on the left a part of our plate 109 (the group in the lower left corner, the fighting horsemen towards the left of a bridge), in the centre plate 108, and on the right Windsor drawing No. 12339 *recto*. Neither reconstruction is quite convincing.[27]

Between 1558 and 1565 Vasari destroyed Leonardo's wall-painting *The Fight for the Standard* by overpainting it with one of his frescoes. Several copies of this battle scene are extant, the best of them in the Uffizi. This copy is not quite complete; it does not show the crouching man in the lower left corner, and also not the lower end

of the painting. This part was probably covered by panelling, or by benches, at the time when the copyist did his work. The engraving in the publication by Séroux d'Agincourt is made from a complete (now missing) copy.

109-110

STUDIES FOR THE BATTLE OF ANGHIARI. Venice, Academy, 215A and 215; 16.1×15.3 cm.; and 14.5×15.2 cm.

A part of the blank paper is not reproduced here. The upper sketch in No. 110 is for the centre part of the cartoon. The lower sketch in No. 109 shows, on the right, an idea for the same part; continued, towards the left, with another scene, *The Fight near the Bridge.* See note on plate 108.

111

STUDY FOR THE TRIVULZIO MONUMENT. Windsor, 12355

Leonardo made preparatory studies for two equestrian monuments: that of Francesco Sforza, from 1483 to 1496, and that of Marshal Giacomo Trivulzio probably 1508 to 1512. The first monument certainly reached the model stage (see Documents, I, item 10; and II-VI). Leonardo intended to adorn the monument with 'six harpies with candelabra'. The horse was to be life-size, so the complete monument – as given in this sketch – would have been about 21 feet high.

The most interesting part of plate 111 are the designs of the elaborate base[28] on which horse and rider were to

27. See also G. Neufeld, *Leonardo da Vinci's Battle of Anghiari: a genetic reconstruction,* in *The Art Bulletin,* XXXI, 1949, p. 170f.; and J. Wilde, *Michelangelo and Leonardo,* in *Burlington Magazine,* 1953, pp. 70-77.

28. A. Venturi, in *L'Arte XVII,* 1914, p. 153 f.

be placed. Neither Donatello's *Gattamelata* nor Verrocchio's *Colleoni* stand on such a triumphal arch; Baroncelli's equestrian monument of 1454 at Ferrara was the only possible model, as Leon Battista Alberti had designed for it a base with arches. Unfortunately this monument was destroyed during the French Revolution.

112–113

STUDIES OF HORSES. Windsor, 12290 and 12321

Kenneth Clark (1954) dates the first of the two drawings correctly 'about 1490–1'. The other drawing is of the same period, and both, according to this date, must be studies for the Sforza monument.

114

HORSE AND RIDER. Bronze statuette, 24 cm. high. (The socle is modern.)

The style of this bronze has been compared to the drawings for *The Fight for the Standard* (plate 108), and with the style of the designs for the Trivulzio monument (plate 111). It is clearly the most Leonardesque of all bronzes attributed to the master.

The rider is cast separately. In his left hand he is holding a shield (not visible in our reproduction); the right hand was holding a sword, which is now lost.

Compare plate VI.

There is a drawing at Windsor (12328), with a note by Leonardo that he should not forget to make small models in wax of the horses and men drawn (plate VIII–a). This note can be connected with the horseman in Budapest (plate 114) and similar bronzes.

A small bronze figure of a man, covering himself with his shield, in the Collection of Principe Trivulzio in Milan, belonged originally either to this or to a similar bronze group. There are other fine bronzes of rearing and of pacing horses: in the Metropolitan Museum, the Frick Collection, the Rijksmuseum, the Berlin Museum, the Paget Collection, London, the Bargello, the Castello Sforzesco, the Wallace Collection, the British Museum, the Jeannerat Collection, London, and in the Collection of Duchessa dell'Arcuella, Naples.

Gian Francesco Rustici (with the help of Leonardo): The Baptist between a
Pharisee and a Levite, 1506–11. Bronze group over the north door of
the Florentine Baptistery.

PLATE V. Gian Francesco Rustici (with the help of Leonardo): *Levite and Pharisee*, from the bronze group *St. John preaching*, 1506–11. Florence, Baptistery (above Ghiberti's first door).

PLATE VI. Gian Francesco Rustici (with the help of Leonardo?): *Battle scene*. Terracotta. About 1508. Florence, Bargello.

PLATE VII. Attributed (by Valentiner) to Leonardo: *Head*, detail of Verrocchio's terracotta relief *Resurrection of Christ*. About 1478. Florence, Bargello.

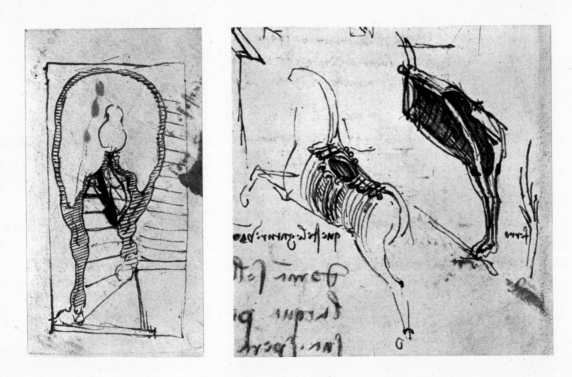

PLATE VIII. (a) Leonardo: *Sketches of men and horses*, with the inscription *"fanne un picholo di cera lũgho un dito"* (make a little wax model after it, one finger long). Detail of a drawing, about 1506. Windsor Castle (No. 12328 r.). – (b) and (c) *Sketches in preparation of casting the Bronze Horse for the Sforza Monument.* 1491–93. Details of two drawings at Windsor Castle. (b) *The Horse within a mould.* – (c) *Two sketches of moulds for casting a prancing horse.*

NOTES ON THE SUPPLEMENTARY PLATES

Plate I. *Paintings by Lorenzo di Credi, supposed to have been painted with the help of Leonardo, or sometimes even attributed to Leonardo himself.* – (a) Madonna and Child with Pomegranate (known as the 'Dreyfus Madonna'). Panel, 16 × 12.6 cm. Berenson lists this picture as by Lorenzo di Credi; the attribution to Leonardo is mainly due to Langton Douglas and Valentiner. The drawing in the Dresden Print Room, considered a preparatory study for this Madonna, is according to Berenson (No. 672) by Credi; according to Langton Douglas by Verrocchio; according to Valentiner by Verrocchio, overdrawn by Lorenzo di Credi. Heydenreich connects the Dreyfus Madonna with the Munich Madonna (plate 63) and contends that the latter was painted in Verrocchio's workshop with the help of Leonardo, the former only under his influence. The description: 'Painted in Verrocchio's studio by Lorenzo di Credi, perhaps assisted by young Leonardo; from the same period as the Pistoia Altarpiece', comes probably very near to the full truth. – (b) A detail from the Pistoia Altar-piece (called 'Madonna di Piazza'). This altar-piece was commissioned from Verrocchio in 1474; in 1478 it was nearly finished; in 1485 it was completed by Lorenzo di Credi. Langton Douglas and Valentiner assumed that Leonardo collaborated in this painting between 1475 and 1478, not only by helping in the painting of the predella but also of the central panel. (See illustration on p. 27. The detail, reproduced as plate I-a, measures in the original 52 × 36 cm.) – (c) and (d) Parts of the Predella of the Pistoia Altarpiece. Panels, about 14 cm. deep. One cannot improve on Berenson's conclusion, who calls the panel in the Louvre 'Lorenzo di Credi, retouched by Leonardo', and the panel in Worcester simply 'by Lorenzo di Credi'.

Plate II. The Sforza portraits in Montorfano's 'Crucifixion'. This attribution rests on Vasari's statement (see p. 17). The figures of the donors Ludovico Moro and his wife, Beatrice d'Este, with their sons Massimiliano and Francesco, in the 'Pala Sforzesca' (Brera; Suida, fig. 15) are rather similar. (See also Document VII, p. 34. Whereas Montorfano's work is well preserved, the Sforza portraits (plate II) have completely flaked off, showing the naked wall and an outline drawing of the figures; they were not painted on top of Montorfano's finished fresco but directly on the wall, which means that a space had been reserved for the portraits. These portraits are probably based on two cartoons, or large drawings, by Leonardo, who certainly had no share in the execution of the painting of the figures (1497–98).

Plate III–a. 'LA BELLE FERRONNIÈRE'. Louvre, No. 1600. Panel; size of this detail, 45 × 34 cm.
The lady wears a small *scuffa*, or cap, on the back of her head, and a *ferronnière* round her brow. (A *ferronnière* is a head-band which originally formed the velvet rim of a hair net, but was later made of gold and ornamented with jewels.) This was a common Lombard fashion.
Claiming it in 1839 as a portrait of Lucrezia Crivelli, Waagen was the first to attribute it to Leonardo. In 1894 Frizzoni was the first to attribute it to Boltraffio. In our time some of the best authorities – including A. Venturi, Berenson, Sir Charles Holmes, Kenneth Clark, and Beltrami – have reverted to the belief in Leonardo's authorship.
We recall a letter, written by Pietro da Novellara in 1501 (Documents, XI) in which he says: 'Leonardo has done nothing else, except that he now and then lends a hand to one or another of the portraits which his two assistants are painting.' Giovanni Antonio Boltraffio, born in 1467, joined Leonardo's studio not later than 1490. But X-ray photographs of the Belle Ferronnière, exhibited side by side with other X-ray photographs of paintings undoubtedly by Boltraffio (Vienna Academy, 1953, Catal. L. Münz, p. 10) proved clearly that not a single brush-stroke in this painting could be from the hand of Boltraffio; nor is anything in it by Leonardo himself. Plate III–a shows the portrait to its best advantage: without the stone breastwork and with a little less of the vast dead background. There is a possibility that the Leonardo pupil who painted this prosaic portrait had the use of a drawing by his master, perhaps similar to plate 25, and certainly less sketchy than plate 5. The indifferent colouring but sensitive shading of the figure is in the manner of Melzi, best known from the sweet heads of his 'Colombine' and 'Pomona' (Bodmer, figs. 89 and 90; Suida, 299 and 302).

Plate III–b. PORTRAIT OF A LADY. Washington, National Gallery, Kress Collection. Panel, 48 × 34.5 cm. The painting was first attributed to Leonardo by Suida (1940) and identified as a portrait of Beatrice d'Este; but the portrait of Beatrice d'Este in the Castello Sforzesco shows a different profile. A variant of the portrait (in the Musée Jacquemart-André, Paris) including both hands, has been identified by Emil Schaeffer (verbally) as a likeness of Beatrice of Portugal, Duchess of Savoy, the sister-in-law of Charles V. The fashion worn by this lady indicates a date of about 1506 (cf. Ō. Fischel, *Raphael*, London, 1946, plate 49).

Plate IV. The Last Supper. See note on plates 71–73.

Plate V. Rustici: *The Baptist between a Pharisee and a Levite*. Florence, Baptistery. (See the illustration on p. 180.) Rustici received the commission for this bronze group towards the end of 1506 and worked on it till September 1509, when he began, with the help of Bernardino da Milano, the casting in bronze. Leonardo stayed in Florence from September 1507 to June 1508, living in Piero di Braccio Martelli's house, in which was also Rustici's studio. In the Life of Baccio Bandinelli, Vasari gives some further information: 'Baccio's father, perceiving his son's bent . . . put the boy in charge of Giovan Francesco Rustici, one of the best sculptors of the city, where Leonardo continually practised. . . . Encouraged by Leonardo's advice, Baccio began to copy an ancient marble head of a woman which he had modelled from one in the Medici palace'. In the Life of Rustici we read: 'Rustici learned much from Leonardo, especially in making horses, of which he was very fond, producing them in clay, in wax, in full and in bas-relief, and every imaginable way. . . . As he lived awhile in the via de' Martelli, he was very friendly with the family'. In the same chapter, Vasari supplies more information about Leonardo's help with Rustici's bronze group over the door of the Florence baptistery: 'While engaged upon this work Rustici would allow no one near save Leonardo da Vinci, who never left him while he was moulding and casting until the work was finished. Many therefore believe, though nothing definite is known, that Leonardo worked at them himself, or at least helped Rustici with his advice and judgement.' I do not believe that Leonardo had anything to do with the central figure, the short-legged, long-armed St John whose drapery is badly designed and modelled; though Rustici might have used Leonardo's drawing of the *Angel of the Annunciation* for the upward pointing right arm. But the Pharisee and the Levite are of a much higher quality than that of anything ever attributed to Rusticci (by Charles Loeser, Kennedy, Middeldorf, and Valentiner).

Plate VI. Rustici: *Battle Scene*. Florence, Museo Nazionale del Bargello. Terracotta, 45.5 cm. high. There are similar terracotta groups by Rustici in the Palazzo Vecchio, and in two private collections in Florence, and in the Camondo Collection of the Louvre. Most of them have been discussed in full by R. Stites (in *Art Studies*, 1926–1931). A similar sculpture is described in a *novella* by Antonfrancesco Grazzini (about 1550): 'In the shop of a terracotta dealer behind San Giovanni, or also in the *bottega* of Verrocchio in the Via del Garbo, a relief is to be seen of a rider on a horse, which kicks and bites four or five men crouching

underneath, while the rider himself wounds one and crushes another. They, however, assail both horse and rider with swords and hatchets, nails and teeth, in the strangest attitudes and wildest contortions.' After Verrocchio's death his *bottega* was carried on and, according to Vasari, Rustici worked there at one time.

Plate VII. *Verrocchio's 'Resurrection of Christ'*, terracotta relief from the Villa Careggi. Florence, Bargello. Valentiner, and others, assume that Leonardo collaborated in this work (see Valentiner, *Studies of Italian Renaissance Sculpture*, London, 1950, p. 166 f.). The detail shown in plate VII should be compared with the 'Head of a Warrior', plate 13. About the *Rattier relief* from Verrocchio's workshop, attributed to Leonardo, see note on plate 3. The marble bust of a *Lady holding Primulas*, usually regarded as a work of Verrocchio, though attributed to Leonardo by Mackowsky, Suida and others, is illustrated on p. 25. A beautiful relief of a *Madonna and Child* (formerly in the Dibblee collection, Oxford; illustrated here), also

Workshop of Verrocchio (attributed to Leonardo by Mackowsky and A. Venturi): *Madonna and Child*, stucco relief, about 1476. London, Mrs. Raymond Johnes.

comes from the Verrocchio bottega. There is another specimen known, of exactly the same size, in the collection of Professor Piero Tozzi, New York (ill. Valentiner, *Studies of Italian Renaissance Sculpture*, fig. 187). Both *stucchi* are obviously taken from the same (lost) marble relief, but the Tozzi relief has been worked over with the knife by some pupil. These stucco versions are, as always has been admitted, based on Verrocchio's *Madonna with the standing Child,* a terracotta relief dating from about 1472–76 (Florence, Bargello). There are great differences between Verrocchio's terracotta relief and the stucco. In the stucco we find a flow of line similar to the *Rattier relief;* the child with his large head and his short legs is rendered in a naturalistic spirit; the heads, and arms, and hands in the stucco version are

dropping in an almost Botticellesque manner, indeed different from Verrocchio's vigorous conception. (See T. Cook, *The Signa Madonna,* London; and A. Venturi in *L'Arte,* 1922.)

Leonardo lived for at least ten years in Verrocchio's house (1469–79); we know from Vasari and Albertini that he painted one angel in his master's *Baptism of Christ*; but we do not know which sculptures from the Verrocchio workshop are partly or completely the work of Leonardo.

Plate VIII. See note on plates 106 and 114.

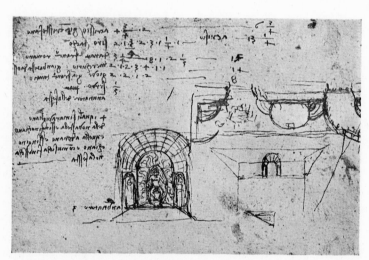

Leonardo: Sketch for the stage setting of Taccone's "Danae", 1496.
New York, Metropolitan Museum.

SHORT BIBLIOGRAPHY

THIS LIST CONTAINS ONLY BOOKS ON LEONARDO AS AN ARTIST

The books and articles are arranged in chronological order

BIBLIOGRAPHY

(1) *Raccolta Vinciana presso l'Archivio Storico del Commune di Milano*, ed. Ettore Verga, since 1905.

(2) Ettore Verga, *Bibliografia Vinciana, 1493–1930.* Bologna 1931 (2 vols.).

(3) *Leonardo Bibliography* in *Raccolta Vinciana* XIV–XVI, Milan 1930–39. (Continuing No. 2.)

(4) *Leonardo Bibliography 1939–1952*, by L. H. Heydenreich, in *Zeitschrift für Kunstwissenschaft*, vol. XV, 1952, pp. 195–200. (Continuing No. 3.)

THE MANUSCRIPTS

A list of all publications of Leonardo's MSS. in Richter, II, pp. 419–42; also Kate T. Steinitz, *The Manuscripts of Leonardo da Vinci* (The Elmer Belt Library of Vinciana), Los Angeles 1948. See also Augusto Mariani, *Leonardo da Vinci, Tutti gli scritti* (I: *scritti letterari*), Milan 1952; and *I manoscritti di Leonardo da Vinci* (in *Saggi e ricerche*, Rome 1954).

(5) E. Solmi, *Le fonti dei manoscritti di Leonardo da Vinci.* Turin 1908.

(6) Gerolamo Calvi, *I Manoscritti di Leonardo da Vinci dal punto di vista cronologico, storico e biografico.* Bologna 1925.

(7) Edward McCurdy, *Leonardo da Vinci's Note-Books.* London 1906. (New edition, in 2 vols., London 1938.)

(8) *The Literary Works of Leonardo da Vinci.* Compiled and edited from the original manuscripts by Jean Paul Richter. Second edition enlarged and revised. 2 vols. Oxford University Press, London and New York 1939.

LEONARDO'S TREATISE ON PAINTING

(9) *Il Trattato della Pittura:* Bibliography 1651–1913, by Aldo Mieli, in *Archivo di storia della scienza* I, 1919–20, p. 177 f.

(10) *Trattato della Pittura di Leonardo da Vinci*, Prefazione di Angelo Borzelli. Lanciano 1914. (The first edition of Leonardo's Trattato was issued in Paris, 1651.)

(11) *Trattato della Pittura*, Italian edition of the Cod. Urbinas Lat. 1270 in the Vatican, with German translation in *Quellenschriften für Kunstgeschichte*, ed. Heinrich Ludwig, 3 vols. Vienna 1882. (Second edition, in German, by Marie Herzfeld, Jena 1909.) Additions: *Das Buch von der Malerei, Neues Material*, ed. H. Ludwig. Stuttgart 1885.

(12) *Treatise on Painting* (Cod. Urbinas Lat. 1270) by Leonardo da Vinci, translated and annotated by A. Philip McMahon, 2 vols. Princeton 1956.

(13) Lionello Venturi, *La Critica e l'Arte di Leonardo da Vinci.* Bologna 1919.

THE DOCUMENTS

(14) Carlo Amoretti, *Memorie storiche sulla vita . . . de Leonardo da Vinci.* Milan 1804.

(15) G. Campori, *Nuovi documenti per la vita di Leonardo da Vinci.* Modena 1865.

(16) G. Milanesi, *Documenti inediti riguardanti Leonardo da Vinci.* Florence 1872.

(17) G. Uzielli, *Ricerche intorno a Leonardo da Vinci:* vol. I, Florence 1872 (second edition, Turin 1896). vol. II, Rome 1884.

(18) N. Smiraglia Scognamiglio, *Ricerche e documenti sulla giovinezza di Leonardo da Vinci.* Naples 1900.

(19) C. Brun, *Die Quellen zur Biographie Leonardos*, in *Festgabe für Hugo Blümmer*, Zürich 1914.

(20) G. Calvi, *Contributi alla Biografia di Leonardo da Vinci*, in *Archivio Storico Lombardo*, 1916, XLIII.

(21) Luca Beltrami, *Documenti e Memorie riguardanti la vita e le opere di Leonardo da Vinci.* Milan 1919.

(22) Aldo de Rinaldis, *Storia dell' opera pittorica di Leonardo da Vinci.* Bologna 1926.

Many documents are quoted in the notes to the Vasari editions by Milanesi, Horne and Poggi (Nos. 26–28). A useful survey, by W. v. Seidlitz, *Regesten zum Leben Leonardos da Vinci*, in *Repertorium f. Kunstwissenschaft* XXXIV, 1911, pp. 448–458.

THE EARLY BIOGRAPHIES

(23) *Libro di Antonio Billi*, ed. Carl Frey, Berlin, 1892. (The earliest life among the Florentine art annalists, named after the merchant who was either the author or the possessor of the book, written about 1518.)

(24) Paolo Giovio, *The Life of Leonardo da Vinci*, in Richter, I, pp. 2–3, Oxford 1939. (Written c. 1527.)

(25) *Anonimo Magliabecchiano (or Gaddiano)*, ed. Carl Frey, Berlin 1892. (Written between 1540–48, derived information from Billi's book and served as a source for Vasari.)

(26) Giorgio Vasari, *Le Vite de' più eccellenti Pittorie, Scultori ed Architettori, con nuove annotazioni e commenti di Gaetano Milanesi.* Vol. IV, Florence 1879. (First edition of Vasari's book 1550, second edition 1568.)

(27) *The Life of Leonardo da Vinci by Giorgio Vasari*, done into English with a commentary by Herbert Horne. London 1903.

(28) Giovanni Poggi, *Leonardo da Vinci, La Vita di Giorgio Vasari nuovamente commentata e illustrata.* Florence 1919 (200 plates).

(29) Antonio de Beatis, *Die Reise des Kardinals Luigi d'Aragona*, ed. L. Pastor, Freiburg 1905. (The Cardinal visited Leonardo at Amboise, in October 1517.)

(30) G. Paolo Lomazzo, *Trattato dell' Arte della pittura*. Milan 1584 (English translation, Oxford 1598).

(31) G. Paolo Lomazzo, *Idea del tempio della pittura*. Milan 1590. (Lomazzo had direct information about Leonardo from Francesco Melzi.)

The Leonardo biographies from Nos. 24, 25 and 26, translated into English, are printed in the present volume; the short note on Leonardo in the Libro di Antonio Billi is analysed on p. 28.

LEONARDO'S APPEARANCE

(32) Luca Beltrami, *Il volto di Leonardo da Vinci*. (Istituto di Studi Vinciani), Rome 1919. (Also in *Emporium*, Bergamo 1919, pp. 3–17.)

(33) Emil Möller, *Wie sah Leonardo aus?* in *Belvedere*, IX, Vienna 1926, pp. 29–46.

(34) L. Planiscig, *Leonardos Porträte und Aristoteles*, in *Festschrift für Julius Schlosser*. Vienna 1927.

(35) Giorgio Nicodemi, *Il volto di Leonardo da Vinci*, in *Leonardo da Vinci* (Mostra, Milan 1939) ed. Istituto Geografico de Agostini, Novara (1939).

BOOKS AND ESSAYS ON LEONARDO'S ART

(36) Carlo Giuseppi Gerli, *Disegni di Leonardo da Vinci incisi e publ*. Milan 1734.

(37) Gabriel Séailles, *Léonard de Vinci, l'artiste et le savant*. Paris 1892. (New edition, Paris 1912.)

(38) Walter Pater, *The Renaissance*. London 1893 (pp. 103–135: Essay on Leonardo).

(39) Paul Müller-Walde, *Leonardo da Vinci: Lebensskizze und Forschungen*. München 1889–90 (unfinished).

(40) Paul Müller-Walde, *Beiträge zur Kenntnis des Leonardo da Vinci*, in *Jahrbuch der preussischen Kunstsammlungen*, Berlin 1897–99.
(I. Ein neues Dokument zur Geschichte des Reiterdenkmals für Francesco Sforza. – II. Eine Skizze zur Leda. – III–IV. Vorbereitungen zum hl. Johannes des Louvre. – Eine frühe Redaktion von Leonardo's Komposition der Madonna mit der hl. Anna und dem Lamm. – VII–VIII. Leonardo und die antike Reiterstatue des Regisole. Entwürfe zum Reiterdenkmal für Trivulzio. Plaketten nach Studien Leonardos zu Reiterdenkmälern und zur Reiterschlacht von Anghiari.)

(41) Edmondo Solmi, *Leonardo*. Florence 1900.

(42) W. v. Seidlitz, *Leonardo da Vinci, der Wendepunkt der Renaissance*, 2 vols. Berlin 1909. (The second edition, very different from the first, Vienna 1935.)

(43) Bernard Berenson, *The Study and Criticism of Italian Art*, III. London 1916 (pp. 1–37: Leonardo da Vinci, an attempt at revaluation).

(44) Osvald Sirén, *Leonardo da Vinci, The Artist and the Man*. New Haven 1916. (Revised French edition, 3 vols., Paris and Brussels 1928. See the review by Sir Eric Maclagan, in *Burlington Magazine*, LIV, 1929, p. 277.)

(45) Giulio Carotti, *Leonardo da Vinci*. Turin 1921.

(46) Wilhelm von Bode, *Studien über Leonardo da Vinci*. Berlin 1921.

(47) A. Schiaparelli, *Leonardo ritrattista*. Milan 1921.

(48) Ettore Verga, *Gli studi intorno a Leonardo da Vinci*. Rome 1923.

(49) Max Dvořák, *Geschichte der italienischen Kunst im Zeitalter der Renaissance: Akademische Vorlesungen* (*Vienna*, 1918–20). Munich, 1927 (vol. I, pp. 143–194: Leonardo.)

(50) Edmund Hildebrandt, *Leonardo da Vinci*. Berlin 1927.

(51) Edward McCurdy, *The mind of Leonardo da Vinci*. London 1928.

(52) Anny A. Popp, *Leonardo da Vinci: Zeichnungen*. München 1928.

(53) *I disegni di Leonardo da Vinci*. Published in facsimile by the R. Commissione Vinciana (A. Venturi). Part I–VII. Rome 1928–52 (252 plates).

(54) Wilhelm Suida, *Leonardo und sein Kreis*. München 1929.

(55) Sir Kenneth Clark, *Leonardo da Vinci: An Account of his development as an artist*. Cambridge 1929. (Revised edition, Penguin books No. A430, London 1958.)

(56) Heinrich Bodmer, *Leonardo: des Meisters Gemälde und Zeichnungen*. Klassiker der Kunst, vol. 37. Stuttgart 1931. (With 360 illustrations.)

(57) Edward McCurdy, *Leonardo da Vinci: The Artist*. London 1933.

(58) Girolamo Calvi, *Vita di Leonardo da Vinci*. Brescia 1936 (second edition, 1949).

(59) Bernard Berenson, *The Drawings of the Florentine Painters*, Amplified Edition, 3 vols. Chicago 1938. (A Catalogue of Leonardo Drawings, vol. II, pp. 109–138; and 99 illustrations in vol. III.)

(60) H. Bodmer, *Disegni di Leonardo* (100 illustrations). Florence 1939 (second edition, 1943).

(61) Odoardo H. Giglioli, *Leonardo. Iniziazione alla connoscenza di Lui e delle questioni Vinciane*. Florence 1944.

(62) R. Langton Douglas, *Leonardo da Vinci*. Chicago 1944.

(63) *The Drawings of Leonardo da Vinci*, with an Introduction and Notes by A. E. Popham. London 1946.

(64) Giorgio Castelfranco: *Leonardo da Vinci*. Milan 1952.

(65) Ludwig Heinrich Heydenreich, *Leonardo da Vinci*, second edition, 2 vols., Basel 1954. (English edition, 1 vol., London 1954.)

LEONARDO'S EARLIEST PERIOD

(66) Sigmund Freud, *Eine Kindheitserinnerung des Leonardo da Vinci*. Vienna 1910. (Also an English translation, by Prof. A. A. Brill.)

(67) Jens Thiis, *Leonardo da Vinci: The Florentine years of Leonardo and Verrocchio*. London (1913). (Swedish edition 1909; revised French edition 1928.)

(68) Sir Charles Holmes, in *Burlington Magazine*, February 1914, *review of Thiis's book on Leonardo*. (About Leonardo's activities in Verrocchio's workshop.)

(69) W. R. Valentiner, *Leonardo as Verrocchio's co-worker*, in

The Art Bulletin (XII, 1), University of Chicago, March 1930, pp. 43–89.

(70) W. R. Valentiner, *Leonardo und Desiderio*, in *Jahrb. d. preuss. Kunstsamml.* LXI, 1932, p. 53 f.

(71) Emil Möller, *Leonardo e il Verrocchio in Raccolta Vinciana* XIV, Milan 1930–4.

(72) Bernard Berenson, *Verrocchio e Leonardo – Leonardo e Credi*, in *Bollettino d'Arte*, 1933–34 (pp. 241–264; 193–213).

(73) Adolfo Venturi, *Leonardo scultore nella bottega del Verrocchio* in *Nuova Antologia*, 1934, March, pp. 34–39; *L'Arte* 1936, pp. 243–265.

(74) W. R. Valentiner, *Über zwei Kompositionen Leonardos*, in *Jahrb. d. preuss. Kunstsamml.*, vol. 56, 1935, p. 213 f.

(75) W. R. Valentiner, *Leonardo's Early Life*, in the 'Catalogue of the Leonardo Exhibition', Los Angeles County Museum, 1949, pp. 43–60.

(76) W. R. Valentiner, *Studies of Italian Renaissance Sculpture*, London 1950 (On Leonardo's Relation to Verrocchio, pp. 113–177. Two Terracotta Reliefs by Leonardo, pp. 178–192.)

(77) Ludwig Baldass, *Zu den Gemälden der ersten Periode des Leonardo da Vinci*, in *Zeitschrift für Kunstwissenschaft*, vol. VII, 3–4, Berlin 1953, pp. 165–182.

LEONARDO THE SCULPTOR

(78) L. Courajod, *Léonard de Vinci et la statue équestre de Francesco Sforza*. Paris 1879.

(79) Fr. Haak, *Zur Entwicklung des italienischen Reiterdenkmals*, in *Zeitschr. f. bild. Kunst*, N.F. VII, 1896, p. 273 f.

(80) Simon Meller, *Die Reiterdarstellungen Leonardos und die Budapester Bronzestatuette*, in *Jahrb. d. preuss. Kunstsamml.*, Berlin 1916, pp. 113–140.

(81) A. Cook, *Leonardo da Vinci, Sculptor*. London 1923. (See the review by Sir Eric Maclagan, in *Burlington Magazine*, XLIII, 1923, II, p. 68 f.)

(82) Francesco Malaguzzi Valeri, *Leonardo da Vinci e la scultura*. Bologna 1922.

(83) Raymond S. Stites, *Leonardo da Vinci, Sculptor*, in *Art Studies*, 1926 (p. 103 f.), 1930 (p. 254 f.), 1931 (p. 289 f.). Cambridge, U.S.A.

(84) Adolfo Venturi, in his *Storia dell'Arte Italiana*, vol. X, 1. Milan 1935.

(85) John Goldsmith Phillips, *The Virgin with the Laughing Child*. (A terracotta statuette in the Victoria and Albert Museum, attributed to Leonardo.) In 'Studies to the History of Art, dedicated to William E. Suida', London 1959, pp. 146–153.
See also Nos. 65, 73 and 76.

SINGLE LEONARDO PAINTINGS

(86) 'The Last Supper'. Giuseppe Bossi, *Del 'Cenacolo' di Leonardo da Vinci*. Milan 1810.

(87) Goethe, *Über Leonards da Vinci Abendmahl zu Mailand*, in *Kunst und Alterthum*, III, 1817. (A review of Bossi's book.)

(88) J. Strzygowski, *Leonardos Abendmahl und Goethes Deutung*, in *Goethe-Jahrbuch* 1896, p. 138 f.

(89) Otto Hoerth, *Das Abendmahl des Leonardo da Vinci*. Leipzig 1907.

(90) Luca Beltrami, *Il Cenacolo di Leonardo*. Milan 1908.

(91) Heinrich Wölfflin, *Die Klassische Kunst*; 1898, 6th ed. Munich 1914 (pp. 23–42: analysis of the composition of four Leonardo paintings – Last Supper, Mona Lisa, St Anne, Battle of Anghiari). English edition, Phaidon Press, 1955.

(92) Salomon Reinach, *La Tristesse de Mona Lisa*, in *Bulletin des Musées de France*. Paris 1909.

(93) Luca Beltrami, *Leonardo da Vinci e la Sala delle Asse*. Milan 1902.

(94) M. Lessing, *Die Anghiarischlacht des Leonardo da Vinci*. Bonn 1935.

(95) K. F. Suter, *Leonardos Schlachtenbild*, Strasburg 1937.

(96) Emil Möller, *Das Abendmahl des Lionardo da Vinci*. Baden-Baden 1952.

DRAWINGS IN INDIVIDUAL COLLECTIONS

Florence, Uffizi.

(97) Pasquale Nerino Ferri, *Catalogo riassuntivo della raccolta di disegni antichi e moderni della R. Galleria degli Uffizi di Firenze*. Rome 1890.

(98) Giovanni Poggi, *Drawings by Leonardo da Vinci*. (The drawings of the Royal Gallery of the Uffizi in Florence, published by Leo S. Olschki, fifth series, third portfolio; 20 plates.) Florence 1922.

London, British Museum.

(99) *I manoscritti e i disegni di Leonardo da Vinci, Il Codice Arundel* 263; ed. R. Commissione Vinciana, Rome 1923–30. (Four parts.)

(100) *Italian Drawings, The fourteenth and fifteenth centuries* (Catalogue) by A. E. Popham and Philip Pouncey, 2 vols. London 1950.

Milan, Ambrosiana.

(101) S. Dozio, *Degli scritti e disegni di Leonardo da Vinci all'Ambrosiana*. Milan 1871.

(102) Giovanni Piumati, *Il Codice Atlantico di Leonardo da Vinci nella Biblioteca Ambrosiana*. Milan 1894–1904.

(103) L. Beltrami, *Disegni di Leonardo e della sua scuola alla Biblioteca Ambrosiana*. Milan 1904.

(104) Carlo Pedretti, *Studi Vinciani*, Geneva 1957.

(105) Carlo Pedretti, *Leonardo da Vinci: Fragments . . . from the Codex Atlanticus*. London 1957.

Milan, Brera.

(106) Francesco Malaguzzi Valeri, *I disegni della R. Pinacoteca di Brera*. Milan 1906.

Milan 1939, Leonardo Exhibition.

(107) *Catalogo della Mostra di Leonardo da Vinci*. Milan 1939.

(108) Leonardo da Vinci, *Pubblicazione promossa dalla mostra di Leonardo da Vinci, Milano*. Novara 1939. (English edition, London 1957.)

Paris, Louvre.

(109) L. Demonts, *Les dessins de Leonardo da Vinci au Musée du Louvre.* Paris 1922.

Oxford.

(110) Sidney Colvin, *Drawings of the old Masters in the University Galleries and in the Library of Christ Church, Oxford,* 3 vols. Oxford 1907.

(111) *Catalogue of the Collection of Drawings in the Ashmolean Museum* (vol. II: Italian Schools) by K. T. Parker. Oxford 1956.

Turin, Library.

(112) Pietro Carlevaris, *I disegni di Leonardo da Vinci della Biblioteca di S. M. di Torino.* Turin 1888.

Venice, Accademia.

(113) Gino Fogolari, *I disegni della R. Galleria dell' Accademia di Venezia.* Milan 1913.

Windsor Castle.

(114) Sir Kenneth Clark, *A Catalogue of the drawings of Leonardo da Vinci . . . at Windsor Castle.* Cambridge 1935, 2 vols.

MISCELLANEA

(115) Victor Mortet, *La mésure de la figure humaine et le canon des proportions d'après les dessins de Villard de Honnecourt, d'Albert Dürer et de Léonard de Vinci.* 'Melanges Chatelain', Paris 1910.

(116) O. Münsterberg, *Leonardo und die chinesische Landschafts-malerei,* in *Orientalisches Archiv,* 1911.

(117) Francesco Malaguzzi Valeri, *La Corte di Ludovico il Moro.* Milan 1915 (vol. II, Bramante e Leonardo).

(118) Luca Beltrami, *La destra mano di Leonardo da Vinci.* Milan 1919.

(119) Giambattista de Toni, *Le piante e gli animali in Leonardo da Vinci.* Bologna (1922).

(120) Emil Möller, *Salai und Leonardo da Vinci* in *Jahrbuch d. Kunsthist. Samml. in Wien.* Vienna 1928, pp. 139–161.

(121) A. Baldacci, *Le piante e la pittura di Leonardo da Vinci.* Bologna 1930.

(122) A. Blum, *Léonard de Vinci, Graveur,* in *Gazette des Beaux-Arts,* 1932, p. 88 f. (with bibliography).

(123) Paul Valéry, *Introduction to the method of Leonardo da Vinci,* translated from the French by Thomas McCreevy. London 1929.

(124) Paul Valéry, *Les divers essais sur Léonard de Vinci, commentés et annotés par lui-même.* Paris 1931.

(125) Giuseppina Fumagalli, *Eros di Leonardo.* Milan 1952.

(126) G. Castelfranco, *Il concetto di forza di Leonardo,* in Proporzioni III, 1950, p. 117 f.

(127) Ludwig Goldscheider, *Leonardo da Vinci: Landscapes and Plants.* London 1952.

(128) Joseph Gantner, *Leonardos Visionen von der Sintflut und vom Untergang der Welt.* Bern 1958.

INDEX TO BIBLIOGRAPHY

INDEX OF COLLECTIONS